CENTRAL APENNINES
OF ITALY

The "Canalone Chiaretti - Pietrostefani"
snow gully on the North-east face of Monte Terminillo

CENTRAL APENNINES
OF ITALY
Walks, Scrambles & Climbs

by

Stephen Fox

CICERONE PRESS
MILNTHORPE, CUMBRIA

Acknowledgements

I would like to thank everyone who has helped me in the preparation of this guidebook, especially Maurizio Moras, Wilson Volpicelli, Maurizio Posati, Luigi Mario, Andrea Di Bari, Gustavo Pierangelini, Fabrizio Cappannini, Roan Fair, Marco Francia, and my father, Phil Fox.

ADVICE TO READERS

Readers are advised that whilst every effort is taken by the author to ensure the accuracy of this guidebook, changes can occur which may affect the contents. A book of this nature with detailed descriptions and detailed maps is more prone to change than a more general guide. New fences and stiles appear, waymarking alters, there may be new buildings or eradication of old buildings. It is advisable to check locally on transport, accommodation, shops etc, but even rights-of-way can be altered, paths can be eradicated by landslip, forest clearances or changes of ownership. The publisher would welcome notes of any such changes for future editions.

Front cover: East face of Pizzo del Diavolo

CONTENTS

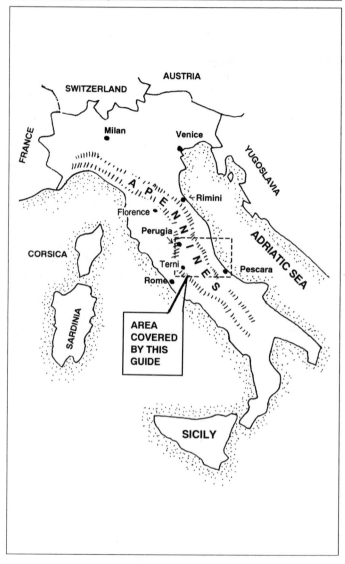

INTRODUCTION

Over one thousand kilometres long, but rarely exceeding one hundred kilometres in width, the Apennines constitute the mountainous 'spine' of the Italian peninsula crossing thirteen of Italy's twenty regions.

The central Apennines cover four of these regions - Abruzzo, Lazio, Marche and Umbria. Here walkers can find secluded valleys and waterfalls, mystical gorges and beautiful woodland, easy mountain excursions and vast plains. Rock climbers and scramblers head for Gran Sasso d'Italia which boasts the giant, pyramidal 'Paretone' wall that towers above plains and farmland of Teramo, only a stone's throw from the Adriatic coast. Corno Piccolo (2655m) is a rock climber's paradise offering an abundance of very good routes from grade III to VIII.

In winter, the central Apennines assume the character of the Alps, offering a number of challenging snow gullies and some mixed ground in the Gran Sasso/Laga and Monti Sibillini National Parks.

Ferentillo and Grotti, situated to the west of the 'spine', are certainly two of Italy's finest sport climbing venues and the mild climate hereabouts makes it possible to climb throughout the year.

GENERAL INFORMATION

1. GRADING OF WALKS, SCRAMBLES AND CLIMBS

Walks

Every walk is graded according to its overall difficulty:

Grade 1 - Refers to routes mostly on good footpaths and/or up gentle slopes that can be attempted by any reasonably fit person.

Grade 2 - Refers to routes that are suited to confident walkers who can find the way when footpaths become indistinct or non-existent. Steep slopes may often be encountered.

Rock Climbs and Winter Climbs

The rock climbs and winter climbs in this guidebook have different gradings. They are:

F (easy), PD (not very hard), AD (fairly hard), D (hard), TD (very hard), ED (extremely hard), EX (exceptionally hard).

Climbs that fall between two grades receive a plus or minus sign depending on the difficulties of the routes. The overall grading for each rock climb reflects a free ascent, even if in situ protection (slings, pitons, etc.) may be found on most routes. All rock passages are outlined following the UIAA's adoption of Roman numerals (III, IV, etc.) and the maximum difficulty is also given, eg. AD+ (max. IV). Occasionally the word *clessidra* will appear in the rock climbing descriptions. This is an Italian word for a rock handle usually shaped like an hourglass with a gap behind it, thus allowing a climber the chance to thread a sling around the handle. *Clessidre* are often encountered on the limestone walls of Gran Sasso and so you will often find old slings already hanging from them. However, you should still take a selection of nuts, camming devices, slings, karabiners, etc. There are so many choice rock routes in the Gran Sasso area that I hope the 'top twenty' I have selected for this guidebook will serve as an interesting and rewarding introduction. I have purposely concentrated on the middle grades (AD, D, TD climbs) and the limestone is nearly always excellent and compact.

The twelve winter climbs (mostly gullies) are perhaps the best known and most frequently climbed in this part of Italy. However, this certainly does not mean you will have to queue at the start of a route - on weekdays you rarely meet other climbers.

Scrambles

Scrambles have rock passages of grade I and / or II and perhaps the aid of ladders and fixed ropes in places. They are graded S I / II in this book.

The scrambles are all situated in the Gran Sasso area in Abruzzo.

Sport Climbing

French grades are used for all climbs in this section (6a, 6a+, 6b, etc.). All of the sport routes in this guidebook have lower-off points and bolts that are regularly checked. They are always listed left to right as you look at the wall in question. The length of each route is given.

2. ROUTE DESCRIPTIONS

The terms L and R (left and right) are always used with reference to the direction of movement of the walker, scrambler or climber. Other abbreviations include N (North), S (South), E (East), W (West), NE (North East) and so on. The walks and scrambles have round-trip times typical for a party walking / scrambling at normal speed, but these do not allow for rests, water breaks, etc. Total ascents (this also includes any uphill sections on the descents) are given, so that the walker / scrambler can appreciate the demands of the routes. For the winter climbs the overall ascents have been divided under two headings: Approach Ascent (snow plod to the start of the climb) and Climbing (the serious bit!). Each rock climb has a Climb Time and Total Climbing which I think are self-explanatory. Descents follow the routes of ascent unless specified otherwise.

3. WEATHER

Warm clothes and waterproofs should always be carried as strong winds and sudden storms can sometimes occur in the Apennines.

The rock climbs and scrambles are perhaps best attempted between June and October, and the winter climbs are usually in condition from the beginning of January to early April. June to November is the best part of the year for the walks, although snow patches may be encountered on mountain excursions at the end of spring / beginning of summer. The Valnerina walks can be done in any season. A compass and altimeter should be taken on mountain excursions and it is advisable to carry a whistle and first aid kit.

4. MOUNTAIN RESCUE

If you witness an accident, or one is brought to your attention, and you feel sure that it is necessary to seek help, telephone 115 or tell the guardian at the nearest refuge.

Audible distress signal: Shout or whistle SIX times a minute, then wait a minute and begin again. Continue until a response is seen or heard.

Visual distress signal: In daylight wave a light/bright piece of clothing SIX times a minute, wait a minute and then begin again. Continue until a response is seen or heard. At night wave a lighted torch/headtorch SIX times a minute, wait a minute and then begin again until a response is seen or heard.

Response: Three such signals a minute.

Helicopter rescue: Do not request air rescue for accidents that are not serious. If the accident is serious and you DO need help then put BOTH arms up in the air, but do not wave. If you do NOT need help and a helicopter or light plane appears to be taking an interest in you, put only ONE arm up in the air, keeping the other by your side.

5. MAPS

Gran Sasso: Club Alpino Italiano's Gran Sasso d'Italia 1:25,000.
Monti della Laga: Club Alpino Italiano's Monti della Laga 1:50,000.
Monti Sibillini: Club Alpino Italiano's Parco Nazionale dei Sibillini 1:25,000 or Monti Sibillini 1:25,000 (Ed. Multigraphic-Firenze).
Valnerina: I.G.M. 1:25,000 (F138 I NO Ferentillo), (F138 I SO Labro) and (F131 II SE S. Anatolia di Narco). *1:25,000 each.*

6. OTHER GUIDEBOOKS

1. *Vette e Sentieri dell'Appennino Centrale* (ed: De Agostini Gorlich) 1989, by Stefano Ardito.
2. *Monti della Laga* (Societa Editrice Ricerche-C.A.I.) 1990, by Alberico Alesi, Maurizio Calibani and Antonio Palermi.
3. *Guida dei Monti Sibillini* (C.A.I.) 1983, by Maurizio Calibani and Alberico Alesi.
4. *Parco Nazionale Gran Sasso - Laga* (BAG editrice s.r.l.) 1993, by Giampiero Di Federico.

5. *Gran Sasso d'Italia* (C.A.I.) 1992, by Luca Grazzini and Paolo Abbate.

6. *Gran Sasso, Arrampicate scelte* (Mediterranee, Roma) 1986, by Roberto Ciato, Furio Pennisi and Bruno Vitale.

7. *Vuoto Compreso*, 1995, by Andrea Di Bari and Simona Bartolucci. A detailed sport climbing guide to Umbria. Can be purchased in Precetto village in the Valnerina.

8. *Escursionismo in Valnerina, nel Ternano e sui M. Martani* (C.A.I. 1991), by Silvano Lepri.

Other useful sources of information
1. *ALP* magazine. Back numbers 4, 31 and 92 are especially useful. Numbers 4 and 31 look at climbing in the Gran Sasso area and number 92 has an interesting article regarding winter climbing in the Monti Sibillini National Park. For information on how to obtain back numbers, write to: Vivalda Editori srl, via Invorio 24a, 10146 Torino, Italy.

7. REFUGES
Monti Sibillini
1. Rifugio degli Alpini (Forca di Presta / 1536m) - open 15/6 to 15/9 and weekends in the winter (tel. 0736/809278). Run by Gino and Daniela Quattrociocchi.

2. Rifugio del Fargno (Forcella del Fargno / 1811m) - open permanently in August, Sundays from June to November (tel. 0733/32071).

3. Rifugio Casali (Casali / 1080m) - open 15/6 to 15/9, 23/12 to 6/1, Easter and weekends. This refuge, run by Paolo Sertelli, was built in 1994 and has 24 beds (tel. 0737/99590 or 0733/433681).

4. Rifugio Taverna della Montagna (Foce / 945m) - open throughout the year (tel. 0736/856327).
   Unfortunately, the tiny Rifugio Zilioli (Monte Vettore / 2233m) is locked now because of past vandalism.

Gran Sasso - Laga
1. Rifugio Franchetti (2433m) - open 1/7 to 15/9. It is run by Luca Mazzoleni and has 20 beds (tel. 0861/959634).

2. Rifugio Garibaldi (2230m) - built in 1886 and recently restored, it has a room that is open throughout the year and another closed with 15 beds; the key to this can be obtained from the C.A.I. office in L'Aquila (Via XX settembre 15, tel. 0862/24342).
3. Rifugio di Campo Imperatore (Campo Imperatore/2130m) - new refuge open throughout the year (tel. 0862/400011).
4. Rifugio Duca degli Abruzzi (2388m) - now that the new, larger Rifugio di Campo Imperatore has been opened, this old refuge is only open discontinuously in the summer.
5. Bivacco Bafile (situated at 2669m on the SE ridge of Corno Grande's central summit) 9 places, useful bivvy hut for climbers and scramblers, permanently open.

Monte Terminillo
1. Rifugio Sebastiani (1820m) - open throughout the year (tel. 0746/261184).

8. CAMPSITES

Monti Sibillini
1. Camping a Lago in San Lorenzo a Lago, Fiastra. Open 15/6 to 15/9 (tel. 0737/52468).
2. Camping Estate/Inverno Il Quercione in Calcara, near Ussita. Open throughout the year. Bungalows (max. 4 persons per bungalow) can be rented here, too (tel. 0737/99448).
3. Monte Prata near Castelsantangelo sul Nera. Open 15/6 to 15/9 (tel. 0737/98124).
4. Camping Montespino, 3km south of Montefortino. Open throughout the year, but full services only from 1/7 to 8/9. Bungalows can be rented.

Gran Sasso
1. Camping Funivia del Gran Sasso at Fonte Cerreto (1120m) near the Gran Sasso cable-car station. Open 1/6 to 15/9 (tel. 0862/606163 or 606586).
    It is still possible to camp in the woods around Prati di Tivo, although it might be wise to inform the local police (Carabinieri office at Pietracamela, 6km N of Prati di Tivo) before doing so.

Certain things are obviously not tolerated, however, like making fires, picking flowers, etc. Please respect the national park regulations.

Valnerina and Ferentillo
1. Scheggino - 10km N of Ferentillo (open 1/6 - 30/9).
2. Marmore - 7km E of Terni (open 1/5 - 30/9).
3. Piediluco - 12km E of Terni (open 1/5 - 30/9).

9. HOTELS

Monti Sibillini
1. Elena, via G. Rossi 20, Visso (tel. 0737/95321).
2. Park, via Battisti 60, Visso (tel. 0737/9218).
3. Bove, Frontignano (tel. 0737/90110).
4. Domus Laetitiae, Frontignano (tel. 0737/90140).
5. Felicita, Frontignano (tel. 0737/90121).
6. Mark, Frontignano (tel. 0737/90193).
7. Crystal di Spuri, via Pie la Costa, Sasso, Ussita (tel. 0737/99415).
8. Ussita, via Fluminata, Ussita (tel. 0737/99521).
9. La Fiorita Spina, near Forca di Gualdo, Castelsantangelo sul Nera (tel. 0737/970064).
10. La Baita, Monte Prata, near Forca di Gualdo (Castelluccio/ Castelsantangelo sul Nera) (tel. 0337/6869545).
11. Carlini, via Roma 18, Montemonaco (tel. 0736/856127).
12. Orsa Maggiore, via Roma 1, Montemonaco (tel. 0736/856128).
13. Taverna della Montagna, Foce (tel. 0736/856327)
14. Albergo Vettore, Balzo, Montegallo (tel. 0736/806458).
15. Regina Giovanna, via Salaria 5, Arquata del Tronto (tel. 0736/ 809148).

Monti della Laga
1. Italia, Acquasanta Terme (tel. 0736/801269).
2. Terme, Acquasanta Terme (tel. 0736/801263).
3. Roma, Amatrice (tel. 0746/85035)
4. Il Castagneto, Amatrice (tel. 0746/85722).
5. Julia, Ceppo (tel. 0861/63100).
6. Monte Gorzano, Padula (tel. 0861/64103).

Gran Sasso

1. Amorocchi, Prati di Tivo (tel. 0861/959603 or 959611).
2. Europa, Prati di Tivo (tel. 0861/959656 or 959630).
3. Gran Sasso, Prati di Tivo (tel. 0861/955109 or 955111).
4. Gran Sasso 3, Prati di Tivo (tel. 0861/959639 or 959669).
5. La Gran Baita, Prati di Tivo (tel. 0861/959604).
6. Miramonti, Prati di Tivo (tel. 0861/859647 or 959657).
7. Orso Bianco, Prati di Tivo (tel. 0861/959625).
8. Prati di Tivo, Prati di Tivo (tel. 0861/959636).
9. Hotel Campo Imperatore, Campo Imperatore (tel. 0862/400000).
10. Fiordigigli, Base Funivia Gran Sasso, Fonte Cerreto (tel. 0862/606173 or 606171).

Grotti

1. Quattro Stagioni, piazza Battisti 14, Rieti (tel. 0746/271071).
2. Flash, via Salvatori 4, Rieti (tel. 0746/296471).

Terminillo

1. Al Cavallino Bianco, Terminillo (tel. 0746/261124).
2. Sporting Hotel Tre Cime, Piazza Campoforogna, Terminillo (tel. 0746/261079).

Valnerina and Ferentillo

1. Ninfa del Nera, Sambucheto, 5km N of Ferentillo (tel. 0744/780172).
2. Rossi, CasteldilLago, 6km S of Ferentillo (tel. 0744/388372).
3. Brenta 2, via Montegrappa 51, Terni (tel. 0744/273957).

10. FAUNA AND FLORA

In remote areas of the central Apennines boars and wolves still roam, although the chance of seeing any are slight. Foxes, hares, badgers, weasels, beech-martens, porcupines and wildcats are more widespread as are buzzards, sparrowhawks, barn owls, eagle owls and kestrels. There are also a number of pairs of golden eagles. An extremely rare crustacean, the *Chirocephalus marchesonii* phyllopod, can still be found in the waters of Lago di Pilato, a small lake situated high in the hills in a picturesque corrie below Monte Vettore (2476m) in the Monti Sibillini National Park.

Regarding the flora of the central Apennines, beech, holm-oak and maple woods are very common and the following flowers (Latin names given) can be seen in the more mountainous areas: *Tulipa australis, Gentiana, Narcissus poeticus, Polygonum bistorta, Papaver alpinum, Dianthus carthusianorum* and the beautiful *Leontopodium nivale* (Apennine edelweiss). The vast Plain of Castelluccio in the Monti Sibillini grants one of the most stunning natural spectacles in Italy at the beginning of summer when a magnificent patchwork of blue, red, yellow and violet flowers appears below the highest mountain in Umbria, Cima del Redentore.

11.   CLIMBING HISTORY

18 May 1420 - Antoine De la Sale climbs Monte Sibilla (2173m)

August 1573 - Francesco De Marchi climbs Corno Grande's west summit (2912m), the highest point in the Apennines.

30 July 1794 - Orazio Delfico climbs Corno Grande's east summit (2903m).

16 July 1807 - P. Spadoni climbs Monte Vettore (2476m), the highest peak in the Sibillini range.

4 March 1876 - Damiano Marinelli, G. Cicoria and Angelo Capocci make the first winter ascent of Monte Vettore.

8 September 1887 - Enrico Abbate and Giovanni Acitelli climb Corno Piccolo (2655m).

1892 - Giovanni Acitelli and Orlando Gualerzi climb Corno Grande's central summit (2893m).

8 February 1893 - Acitelli, Abbate, Gualerzi and Ignazio Carlo Gavini make first winter ascent of Corno Piccolo.

August 1910 - Two Austrians, Hans Schmidt and H. Riebeling, traverse Corno Grande's three summits.

1925 - Ernesto Sivitilli founds the *Aquilotti del Gran Sasso* (The Eaglets), preceding the more famous *Ragni di Lecco* (The Spiders of Lecco) and the *Scoiattoli di Cortina* (The Squirrels of Cortina).

20 September 1934 - Bruno Marsilii and Antonio Panza climb the North face of Monte Camicia (2564m). Dubbed "the Eiger of the Apennines", this face is a maze of rock walls, corridors, gullies and ledges. The face sees very few ascents.

13 September 1959 - Luigi Mario, a very young Italian climber, and Emilio Caruso put up a strong TD+ route on the huge Paretone

(North-East face) of Corno Grande. Considered to be a climb way ahead of its time, the Via Mario - Caruso remained unrepeated for almost twenty years.

Late 1970s - Pierluigi Bini puts up a lot of interesting routes in Gran Sasso and solos quite a few, too!

February 1980 - Giampiero Di Federico makes the first winter solo ascent of Via Alessandri (TD-) on the Paretone face of Corno Grande.

30 September 1982 - Marco Florio solos the Via Classica Marsilii - Panza, North face of Monte Camicia.

4 August 1986 - Baphomet (EX-) created by Paolo and Roberto Caruso.

Summer 1987 - Il Nagual e la Farfalla (EX) created by Paolo Caruso, Giulia Baciocco and Andrea Sarchi.

1990 - Luca Grazzini and Alfredo Massini climb Kronos (EX-), Baphomet (EX-), Golem (ED-) and Emanuela (TD) in one day.

12. PRATI DI TIVO CHAIR-LIFT

If for any reason the chair-lift is not in operation, I recommend driving E from Prati di Tivo to Piana del Laghetto (1650m) where the road ends and then walking up the grassy ridge on your R (Arapietra) via a path to La Madonnina (2015m / 1hr).

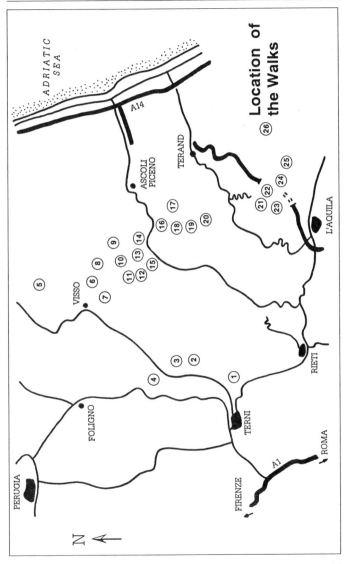

Walks

Valnerina - situated between Terni (Umbria) and Visso (Marche), SS 209 road.

Monastero (Marche) - 13km NW of Sarnano, 10km NE of Fiastra.

Casali (Marche) - 5km E of Ussita, 10km E of Visso.

Frontignano (Marche) - 9km S of Ussita.

Montefortino (Marche) - 6km S of Amandola.

Castelluccio (Umbria) - 22km SE of Visso.

Foce (Marche) - 10km W of Montemonaco.

Acquasanta Terme (Marche) - 18km SW of Ascoli Piceno.

Ceppo (Abruzzo) 37km W of Teramo.

Amatrice (Lazio) - 4km E of the SS 4 (Rieti to Ascoli Piceno) road, 23km S of Arquata del Tronto.

Prati di Tivo (Abruzzo) - 6km S of Pietracamela, 25km SW of Montorio al Vomano (Teramo).

Albergo di Campo Imperatore (Abruzzo) - 27km drive from Fonte Cerreto (SS 17 bis) situated near Assergi. Cable-car service from Fonte Cerreto. Reach Assergi junction on A 24 motorway, 17km from L'Aquila.

Castelli (Abruzzo) - 10km E of Isola del Gran Sasso d'Italia (A 24 motorway junction "Colledara").

1: Cascata delle Marmore

Location:	Valnerina
Grade:	1
Time:	1hr 15mins
Total ascent:	200m
Total distance:	2.5km

Character: This impressive waterfall drops a total of 540 feet and has inspired many poets over the centuries. Shelley wrote: "It comes in

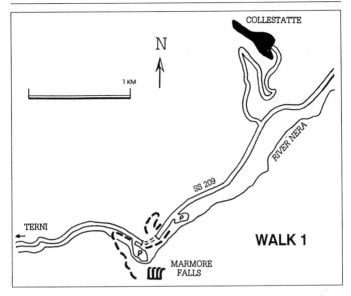

thick and tawny folds, flaking off like solid snow gliding down from a mountain" and Byron referred to it as "a parent of rivers…a matchless cataract."

NOTE: The Marmore Falls can only be seen at certain times of the day. There is a noticeboard with the times to the R of the tunnel. In summer:

Monday to Friday:
    1/6 to 30/6; 1/9 to 30/9 - 3pm to 4.30pm
    1/7 to 31/8 - 11am to 12.30pm and 5pm to 6.30pm
Saturdays:
    1/5 to 31/8 - 11am to 12.30pm and 5pm to 10pm
Sundays and holidays:
    1/5 to 31/8 - 10am to 1pm and 3pm to 9.30pm

Route: From Terni (southern Umbria) drive 6km up the SS 209 (Valnerina) road to the parking area on the R side of the road just before a road tunnel. Beyond this parking area is the Cascata delle Marmore waterfall. Walk 200m back down the SS 209 and turn L down a track that goes under a bridge and leads to an open area

21

Cascata delle Marmore

(metal bridge on the L). Cross this open area and take the evident path that climbs to the R of a solitary house and then R at a fork immediately after. The path leads up through woods and passes through an arch into a grotto before another fork. Go L here along a 60m tunnel (a torch may be useful, but is not entirely necessary) at the end of which there is a small balcony overlooking a lower section of the falls. Returning to the fork, take the other path (steps) up to the main balcony which affords an excellent view of the upper falls (40mins). Walk back down to the parking area (20mins) and take the path between the road tunnel and the falls round to where the SS 209 exits the tunnel. Before reaching another parking area on the R, walk across the road to reach the path that leads up to the balcony in front of the falls above the road tunnel (15mins). The start of this path is marked "Belvedere Gmelin".

2: Il Fosso di Salto del Cieco

Location:	Valnerina
Grade:	1
Time:	1hr
Total ascent:	100m
Total distance:	3km

Character: A short walk up a beautiful, secluded canyon which affords a view of Castellonalto village perched on the top of a high, rocky wall.

Route: Driving NE up the SS 209 (Valnerina) road, continue on past the turning L for Ferentillo (18km from Terni) and take the next turning R for Precetto and Monteriviso. Follow this road through both of these villages and then continue up past the turnings L for Colle Oliva and Castellone Basso. About 400m after the Castellone Basso turning you will go over a bridge (430m). Park just after this on the R and walk across the road to the obvious path that descends to the R of the stream. Arriving at a fenced pen after 100m, go L here and cross the stream (stepping-stones). The path continues up alongside the stream, crossing it twice before arriving at a low barbed-wire fence in front of a flat, grassy area. Climb over this and walk across the flat area to the L of a low, stone wall. The path keeps

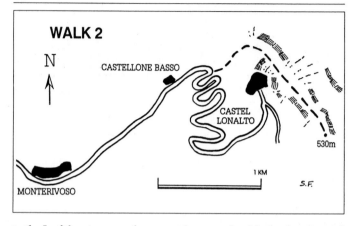

to the L of the stream as far as a rocky mass that blocks the way and here you have to walk a little way up the stream (more stepping-stones) to rejoin the path. There is a small waterfall on the R here and soon after the path narrows and crosses an easy scree slope to the streambed once again. Cross the stream and follow the path to the R of it through a wooded area. At a fork soon after having crossed the stream again, go R along the more evident path (500m) that passes L of another waterfall. The path then comes out of the woods and, passing another waterfall, leads to the stream. From here you can see Castellonalto village high above the canyon walls. Cross the stream and again soon after to reach a fork to the L of a small waterfall. Go R here to the small clearing (530m/35mins). A vague path continues for 1km through areas of dense vegetation, but this part of the canyon is less interesting, so I would suggest turning back at the clearing.

3: Umbriano

Location:	Valnerina
Grade:	1
Time:	1hr 25mins
Total ascent:	125m
Total distance:	3.5km

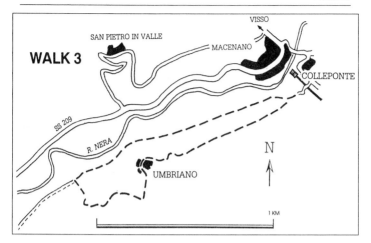

Character: Legend has it that Umbriano was the first village of the Umbrian people. Now completely abandoned, it stands high on a hill overlooking the Valnerina valley directly opposite the Romanesque abbey of San Pietro in Valle. This abbey is the only surviving building from the Duchy of Spoleto.

NOTE: Being an abandoned hill village, Umbriano is a perfect residence for vipers in the hot months (generally May to September). If you decide to do this walk then, it would be wise to carry a *succhia veleno* (snakebite treatment) wallet which can be purchased at most chemists in Italy. Wear proper walking boots that cover the ankles, too.

Route: From Ferentillo in the Valnerina, drive 4km up the SS 209 to the village of Macenano and take the turning R immediately after the severe bend in the village. This side road descends steeply to the hamlet of Colleponte. Cross the bridge over the Nera River and turn immediately R past some houses and a high, stone wall on your R where the road climbs towards a cemetery. Park 100m up this incline on the L opposite another bridge (260m). Walk across this and past some houses (no. 8, 9, 10, 10a) whereafter the road turns into a track. Go R at the first fork. This track passes a spring and then keeps to the L of a stream that soon after joins up with the Nera River. Hereabouts the track can be quite muddy and there are large

25

The Abbazia San Pietro in Valle
which can be seen from the abandoned village of Umbriano

puddles that cannot be skirted. Reaching an evident red pylon, leave the valley track and go L up a narrower one that is quite steep at the start. This then becomes a narrow path that traverses the hillside towards Umbriano and passes a spring (340m); there is a good view of Umbriano from here. Continue along this path and go L at a fork (360m) to reach the derelict village (385m/1hr). Walk through it to the far side and follow the narrow path E down through woods. Thereafter take the descending track at each fork to arrive back at the first fork encountered at the start of the walk and continue on down past the houses and over the bridge again (25mins).

4: The Old Valnerina-Spoleto Railway Line

Location:	Valnerina
Grade:	1
Time:	4hrs 30mins
Total ascent:	325m
Total distance:	15km

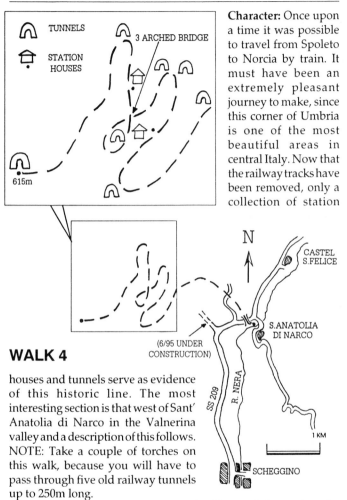

Character: Once upon a time it was possible to travel from Spoleto to Norcia by train. It must have been an extremely pleasant journey to make, since this corner of Umbria is one of the most beautiful areas in central Italy. Now that the railway tracks have been removed, only a collection of station

WALK 4

houses and tunnels serve as evidence of this historic line. The most interesting section is that west of Sant' Anatolia di Narco in the Valnerina valley and a description of this follows. NOTE: Take a couple of torches on this walk, because you will have to pass through five old railway tunnels up to 250m long.

Route: From Terni drive 35km up the SS 209 (Valnerina) to the turning R for Sant' Anatolia di Narco (315m) which comes just after passing under an old railway bridge. Park near the turning (290m) and follow the path across the old railway bridge. Cross an asphalt

27

road after 15mins and continue along the wide path to a bridge over a stream (340m) and the first tunnel (closed to the public). Go L of the tunnel following a vague path that traverses the slope and becomes more evident thereafter. Three tracks meet at 360m - take the one in the middle that leads to the second tunnel which is about 250m long. Walk through this and past an old station house (Number 10) complete with bread oven on the L (415m). Two more tunnels follow in quick succession, both of which are about 100m long (1hr from SS 209 road). The fifth tunnel (about 200m) begins below a three-arched bridge that you will soon walk across after coming out of the tunnel. After the bridge there is another station house (510m) to the R of the path this time. The sixth and shortest tunnel comes before a long traverse of the hillside below an isolated tower to the entrance of the Caprareccia tunnel (615m / 1hr 30mins). This marks 'the end of the line' as it were. It is possible to continue along the railway line all the way to Spoleto, but the Caprareccia tunnel is 2km long and the Spoleto section is not as interesting as that in the Valnerina.

5: Valle del Fiastrone

Location:	Monti Sibillini National Park
Grade:	1
Time:	2hrs 45mins
Total ascent:	360m
Total distance:	7km

Character: Descent to a long, narrow gorge and ascent to a grotto once inhabited by Franciscan hermits.
Route: Reach Monastero (745m) from San Lorenzo a Lago (640m / campsite) and park in the village. Walk back down to the main road (SS 78) and follow it L (NW) for 100m. A grassy path on the N side of the road descends between fields and meets up with a track. Go L down this to the Rio Fessa stream (583m) where the track ends and a path R traverses the hillside to a clearing and then zigzags down through woods to the Fiastrone riverbed where the path forks. Go L here and then L again at a less obvious fork to the narrow gorge

Valle del Fiastrone (at the beginning of the gorge)

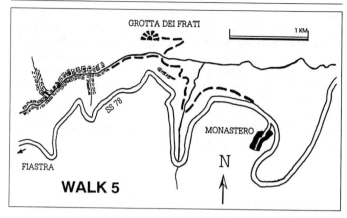

(505m/45mins). Depending on the depth of the stream (wellington boots may be in order), it is certainly worthwhile walking through the gorge which in places becomes a natural tunnel when its walls touch and hanging masses of vegetation spill over them from above. Returning to the first fork encountered after the zigzag descent through the woods, go L now crossing the riverbed by way of a footbridge. Take the path R that zigzags up the hill to a fork and go L here along a good path that traverses the hillside (W) to the Grotta dei Frati (615m/30mins). From this grotto you can see the Fiastrone gorge below.

6: Val di Panico

Location:	Monti Sibillini National Park
Grade:	2
Time:	5hrs 15mins
Total ascent:	885m
Total distance:	11km

Character: This walk offers impressive views of the giant North and East faces of Monte Bove Nord and culminates with a splendid vision of a sea of Sibillini peaks to the south.

Route: From the parking area in front of Casali village church (1080m) follow the track that passes by the church and skirts the N side of the valley for 3km. Before reaching the woods that hug the base of Monte Bove Nord, leave the track near a spring (Sorgenti di Panico - 1285m) and follow the steep path L that climbs the upper valley to a grassy terrace (1550m/1hr 45mins) below a prominent rocky buttress. Go L around this taking an indistinct path that leads up to the grassy ridge above the buttress (1770m). Now follow the ridge faithfully S along an obvious path to Forca della Cervara (grassy col/1965m/1hr 30mins).

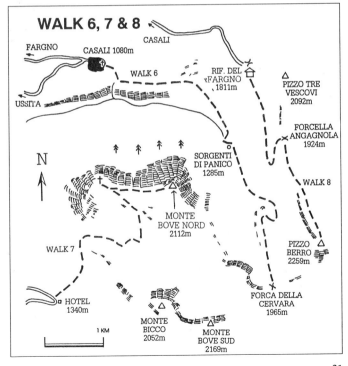

Monte Bove Nord

7: Monte Bove Nord (2112m)

Location:	Monti Sibillini National Park (see Map P31)
Grade:	2
Time:	4hrs 30mins
Total ascent:	822m
Total distance:	8km

Character: Mountain walk offering fine views from the summit of the surrounding valleys.

Route: Go through Frontignano village (winter ski resort) as far as a parking area where the road bends sharply back on itself near the Hotel Felicita (1340m). Take the path that descends E at first through woods and then levels out, slowly turning N until it meets a scree path at 1290m. Go R up this steep scree path to the Val di Bove (1502m/1hr) and continue E along a path to a spring (Fonte di Val di Bove - 1597m). Two paths traverse towards Croce di Monte Bove

---

Il Fosso di Salto del Cieco (Castellonalto village in the background)

Val di Panico (Monte Bove Nord on the right)
Val Tenna

(1905m) which has a large cross on its summit. Take the second, higher path to reach the shoulder just below the summit of Croce di Monte Bove and then go R (E) along the wide, grassy ridge to the summit of Monte Bove Nord (2112m/2hrs).

8: Pizzo Berro (2259m)

Location:	Monti Sibillini National Park (see Map P31)
Grade:	2
Time:	3hrs
Total ascent:	590m
Total distance:	8km

Character: Long ridge walk high above the secluded Val di Panico.
Route: Take the road from Ussita to Casali and just before arriving at Casali go L at a junction (1068m) signposted "Fargno". Drive 13km up this track road to the Forcella del Fargno col (1811m), situated 50m N of the Fargno refuge. Park here and from the refuge head SSE by way of a path that descends and crosses a furrow at 1740m and then levels out for 1km before joining up with a path that comes up from the Val di Panico. At this point take the path L up to the Forcella Angagnola col at 1924m and then follow the mixed grass and rock ridge R (S) up to the summit of Pizzo Berro (2259m/1hr 45mins).

9: **Val Tenna,** La gola dell'Infernaccio

Location:	Monti Sibillini National Park
Grade:	1
Time:	2hrs 40mins
Total ascent:	350m
Total distance:	8.5km

Character: Probably the most spectacular gorge in central Italy. A good, easy path climbs the Val Tenna alongside a rushing torrent

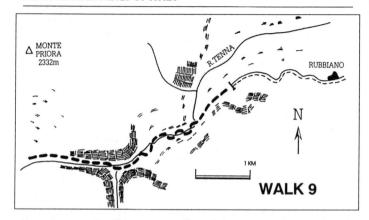

between towering limestone walls and then passes through beech and maple woods. The gorge is narrowest near the start of the walk.
Route: From Montefortino (638m) near Amandola, drive W towards Sossasso and Isola S. Biagio and 2km after the turning for Sossasso go R to Rubbiano (779m) and follow the rough road for 2km where it ends (gate). Park here and continue along the rough road that descends. After 10mins' walk there is a good view of a narrow gorge and waterfall on your R. There is a 200m drop here down to the Tenna torrent. The track leads down to a bridge over the torrent (845m) and a path then climbs into the gorge - La gola dell'Infernaccio. Stay on this path, crossing four more bridges along the gorge to a beech wood where there is an evident fork (940m). Go L here to another bridge below immense, overhanging walls. There is an impressive gorge on your L just before reaching the seventh bridge and a narrow path leads up to this gorge if you want to get a closer look (5mins detour). Cross the seventh bridge and enter more woods, continuing up the main path R at a fork (the path L leads down to the torrent) to an opening where there is another giant gorge to be seen on your L. Continue up to a gap (from here you can see the sky through a hole in the last of the rocky buttresses high above the valley) at 1070m and then descend a little before a long, rising traverse through woods to 1140m where there is a small, stone hut to the R of the path and a spring 100m after this on the L (1130m/1hr 40mins).

Monti Sibillini peaks seen from the summit of Monte Porche

35

10: Monte Porche (2233m), Cima Vallelunga (2221m) and Monte Sibilla (2173m)

Location:	Monti Sibillini National Park
Grade:	2
Time:	5hrs 30mins
Total ascent:	975m
Total distance:	17km

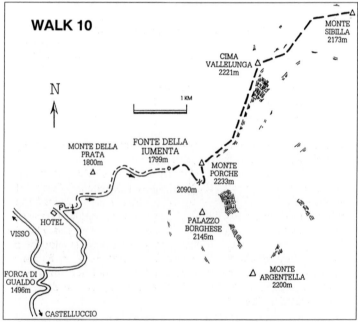

Character: A long walk. An ascent to the top of Monte Porche is followed by a long, airy ridge traverse with wonderful valley views on either side.

Route: From Castelluccio or Castelsantangelo drive to Forca di Gualdo (1496m) where there is the Madonna della Icona chapel and take the road E signposted "Monte Prata" as far as the large parking area called Piazzale Giulio Maurizi (hotel, bar) at 1650m. Park here and follow the evident track E that leads to the Fonte della Iumenta spring (1799m) after 2.5km. Take the steep path that climbs the slope on the other side of the spring to a shoulder and then along the path that traverses the West face of Monte Porche to a col at 2090m. Now go up the S ridge of Monte Porche to its summit (2233m/2hrs). After a brief descent down the NE ridge to 2100m keep to the ridge that undulates all the way to the summit of Cima Vallelunga (2221m) and thereafter to that of Monte Sibilla (2173m/1hr 15mins).

11: Monte Argentella (2200m)

Location:	Monti Sibillini National Park
Grade:	1
Time:	3hrs 30mins
Total ascent:	704m
Total distance:	8km

Character: Easy mountain walk that passes near an interesting monolith called Sasso di Palazzo Borghese.
Route: Drive 3km NE up the track that begins at 1318m below the village of Castelluccio to the C.A.I. refuge (Capanna Ghezzi) at 1570m and park here. Follow the path NE up a grassy slope for 150m where it meets another and go R (SE) up this steeper path to a grassy shoulder (1700m). Take the path L (N) that traverses the grassy West face of Monte Argentella for 2km up to the Passo di Sasso Borghese (2057m). Beyond this col is a monolith called Sasso di Palazzo Borghese. A short descent R (SE) to 2020m is then followed by a gentle ascent slightly R of the NW ridge of Monte Argentella to its summit (2200m/2hrs).

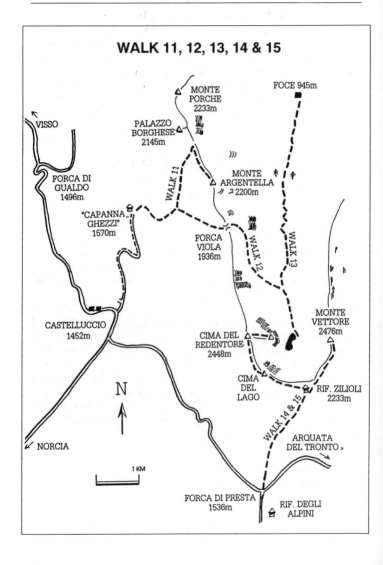

WALK 11, 12, 13, 14 & 15

FOCE 945m

MONTE
PORCHE
2233m

VISSO

PALAZZO
BORGHESE
2145m

WALK 11

MONTE
ARGENTELLA
2200m

FORCA DI
GUALDO
1496m

"CAPANNA
GHEZZI"
1570m

FORCA
VIOLA
1936m

WALK 12

WALK 13

MONTE
VETTORE
2476m

CASTELLUCCIO
1452m

CIMA DEL
REDENTORE
2448m

CIMA
DEL
LAGO

RIF. ZILIOLI
2233m

N

NORCIA

WALK 14 & 15

ARQUATA
DEL TRONTO

1 KM

FORCA DI PRESTA
1536m

RIF. DEGLI
ALPINI

12: Lago di Pilato

Location:	Monti Sibillini National Park (see Map P38)
Grade:	2
Time:	4hrs 30mins
Total ascent:	742m
Total distance:	12km

Character: Scenic excursion that climbs the grassy slopes above the Great Plain of Castelluccio and then drops down into the rugged Valle del Lago di Pilato.

Route: Drive 3km NE up the track that begins at 1318m below Castelluccio village to the C.A.I. refuge (Capanna Ghezzi) at 1570m and park here. Follow the path NE up a grassy slope for 150m where it meets another and go R (SE) up this steeper path to a grassy shoulder (1700m). Avoid the path that goes N and instead take the narrow path R that traverses the SW slope of Monte Argentella as far as an evident furrow. Stay on the L (N) side of the furrow, climbing the short, grassy slope up to the Forca Viola col (1936m/1hr). Descend the steep slope E on the other side following the path that soon traverses the hillside SE as far as Forca di Pala (1852m). The path then traverses a scree slope S to the foot of a rocky buttress, before descending and joining up with a path at 1763m above some ruins (Casaletto). Go R now following the path that leads up to the lake (Lago di Pilato) after 1km (1940m/1hr 30mins).

13: Valle del Lago di Pilato

Location:	Monti Sibillini National Park (see Map P38)
Grade:	1
Time:	5hrs 15mins
Total ascent:	995m
Total distance:	12km

Character: Magnificent walk up one of the most beautiful valleys in the Monti Sibillini National Park.

Route: Drive up the Aso valley to the village of Foce (945m) where the road ends and park. Follow the track that continues up the valley for 2.5km. This track then becomes a path that enters woods below a great rocky buttress on the R known as Ripa Grande and soon steepens, zigzagging its way between rocky masses (le Svolte) to the Valle del Lago di Pilato (1500m/1hr 45mins). The path continues S up the valley to some ruins (Casaletto) at 1748m. Branch L at a fork soon after the ruins and continue along this path to the lake (1940m/1hr 30mins).

14: Monte Vettore (2476m)

Location:	Monti Sibillini National Park
	(see Map P38)
Grade:	1
Time:	4hrs 30mins
Total ascent:	940m
Total distance:	8.5km

Character: The easiest way to the top of the highest peak in the Sibillini area. The path to the Zilioli refuge is quite evident and the view of the rocky Pizzo del Diavolo from the Sella delle Ciaule is spectacular.

Route: Reach Forca di Presta (1536m) from Castelluccio or Arquata del Tronto and park by the side of the wide track that leads S to the Rifugio degli Alpini (1574m). Return to the road and take the path opposite (N) that keeps mostly to the left of the wide, grassy ridge up to 1759m. Cross a grassy terrace here (N) and follow the path up to a second, smaller terrace at 1922m before the Croce Zilioli (a cross erected in memory of Tito Zilioli) situated to the R of the path. Continue along the path that climbs the SW slope of Monte Vettoretto (2052m) to a grassy terrace from where you can see the small Zilioli refuge and Monte Vettore. Follow the obvious path to the Zilioli refuge (2233m), crossing a scree slope (2hrs). Just beyond the refuge is the Sella delle Ciaule (2240m) and from this col go R (E) along the ridge path to the grassy SW slopes of Monte Vettore and the summit (2476m/50mins).

15: Cima del Redentore (2448m) and Pizzo del Diavolo (2410m)

Location:	Monti Sibillini National Park (see Map P38)
Grade:	2
Time:	5hrs 20mins
Total ascent:	950m
Total distance:	11km

Character: Highly recommended ridge walk to the highest mountain in Umbria, Cima del Redentore.

Route: Reach the Zilioli refuge (2233m) from Forca di Presta (see Walk 14: Monte Vettore) and go L (W) up the ridge, keeping a little to the L of it, to Punta di Prato Pulito (2373m/20mins). Cima del Lago (2422m) comes soon after this followed by a brief descent NW and ascent to the top of Cima del Redentore (2448m/30mins). Finally, descend the ridge on your R (E) that soon reaches Pizzo del Diavolo (2410m/10mins).

16: Cascata della Volpara

Location:	Monti della Laga
Grade:	1
Time:	4hrs
Total ascent:	512m
Total distance:	8km

Character: A wonderful walk through woods to one of the more remote waterfalls in the Monti della Laga area.

Route: Reach Umito (640m) from Acquasanta Terme (411m) and take the track R that leads to a little bridge after 1km (668m). Park here and continue along the track for 2km where the track finishes beside a house (830m/45mins). An obvious path takes over, passing through beautiful beech-woods. At 940m there is a fork. Keep to the main path L which zigzags a little before traversing through the

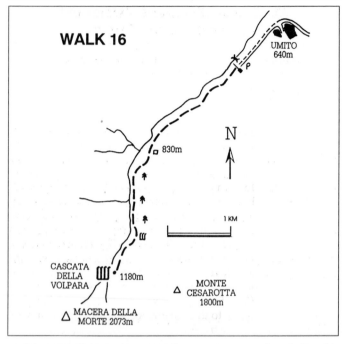

woods and passing two grottoes that were once used as shelters by local woodmen; the second still has an oven by the doorway (40mins). Cross a torrent some 40m before a picturesque waterfall in the woods which can be seen from the path and continue through woodland to the L of the rushing Volpara torrent. Then go R at a fork in an area of dense vegetation and cross two more shallow torrents. Soon after at 1180m, just before the path zigzags steeply through more woods, turn R down a vague path to the Volpara torrent and the lower falls (50mins).

17: Cascata della Morricana

Location:	Monti della Laga
Grade:	1
Time:	4hrs 30mins
Total ascent:	216m
Total distance:	16km

Character: Like the Cascata della Volpara itinerary, this excursion involves a long approach through beautiful woodland to a remote waterfall.

Route: Reach Ceppo (1334m) and take the road S opposite Albergo Julia (hotel) to a fork and park here (1364m). Follow the track R (closed to traffic) through beautiful woodland (Bosco della Martese), avoiding a track on the R that descends steeply after 5km (1hr 10mins). Continue along the main track for 1km where a path takes over and this crosses a torrent (Fosso della Tentazione) before a steep descent. Keep L at a fork soon after and this path continues traversing the L side of the valley, crossing another evident torrent before reaching the Foss V. Castellana torrent below the Morricana waterfall (1580m/1hr 15mins). The walk finishes here, although it is possible to get closer to the waterfall by walking upstream past boulders and fallen tree trunks.

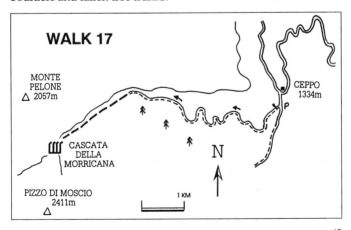

18: Cascata delle Scalette

Location:	Monti della Laga (see Map P45)
Grade:	2
Time:	2hrs 30mins
Total ascent:	425m
Total distance:	6km

Character: A pleasant ascent in open country. Late spring is perhaps the best time to do this walk.

Route: From Amatrice (950m) drive 2km E up the SS 577 and turn L for Retrosi. Drive through Retrosi (1000m) and then turn next R for Ferrazza and San Martino. Park by the church of San Martino (1150m) and walk NE up the track that starts nearby on the bend in the road. Follow this for 2km to its end above a small dam near a cave that can be seen from the track (1400m/50mins). A path continues up the valley and is indicated by a white/red paint mark and the words "Sacro Cuore". Follow the path which climbs L of the stream and then crosses it (stepping-stones) after a small waterfall. A steep path on the other side climbs to a grassy channel N of Monte Dorio (1617m). Go L here over a hillock to a ruin (1575m/yellow paint mark by doorway) and then to some isolated boulders and the slope that leads down to the base of the waterfall (40mins).

19: Cascata delle Barche

Location:	Monti delle Laga (see Map P45)
Grade:	1
Time:	1hr 15mins
Total ascent:	100m
Total distance:	2km

Character: Short, popular walk to a charming waterfall. The last part of the approach may involve getting your feet wet.

Route: From Amatrice (950m) drive 4km E up the SS 577 and turn L for Capricchia (1106m). Continue E along a rough road (yellow

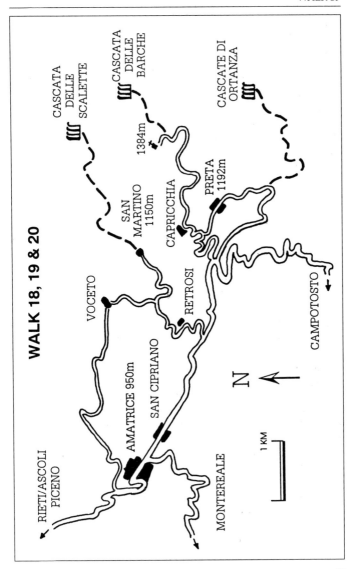

WALK 18, 19 & 20

CASCATA DELLE SCALETTE

CASCATA DELLE BARCHE

CASCATE DI ORTANZA

1384m

SAN MARTINO 1150m

CAPRICCHIA

PRETA 1192m

VOCETO

RETROSI

CAMPOTOSTO

AMATRICE 950m

SAN CIPRIANO

N

RIETI/ASCOLI PICENO

MONTEREALE

1 KM

45

signs for "Gorzano" and "Sacro Cuore") for 3km to a parking/
picnic area some 200m before the Sacro Cuore church (1384m). Park
here and follow the track opposite that enters some woods. After
5mins leave the track and go R up a path that is clearly indicated
"Gorzano" (red/white paint mark on a boulder). Follow this path
out of the woods where it curves L around the hillside and offers a
good view of the rugged S slopes of Cima Lepri (2445m). The path
descends gradually through pleasant woods soon granting a view
of the Barche waterfall. Cross a torrent and follow its course (with
care) down and around to the Barche torrent below the waterfall
(1375m/40mins).

20: Cascate di Ortanza

Location:	Monti della Laga (see Map P45)
Grade:	1
Time:	2hrs 30mins
Total ascent:	310m
Total distance:	6km

Character: The walk up the track is slightly monotonous, but the
ascent through the pine and beech woods to this secluded waterfall
afterwards is quite the contrary.
Route: From Amatrice (950m) drive 4km E up the SS 577 and take
the second turning L on the bend in the road for Preta (1192m). Go
over a bridge above the Tronto River (1km before Preta) and park
on the R where a track (white/red paint mark at the end of the
bridge) begins. Walk up this for 1.5km as far as a grassy terrace in
front of a pine wood; there are red/.white indications on two trees
at the edge of this wood (45mins). Take the path that begins about
10m to the R of the marked tree on the R and turn L after only 150m
(3mins). This path zigzags up through the pine woods and then
traverses a beech wood before crossing two gullies and reaching the
Ortanza torrent above a waterfall (1460m/40mins). You can see the
Ortanza falls upstream and intrepid explorers can get closer still by
clambering over boulders on the L side of the torrent.

21: Val Maone

Location:	Gran Sasso d'Italia
Grade:	1
Time:	3hrs 15mins
Total ascent:	550m
Total distance:	9km

Character: The atmosphere is decidedly Alpine as you walk past huge boulders in the grassy Val Maone below the towering rocky buttresses of Pizzo d'Intermesoli.

Prima Spalla seen from the Val Maone

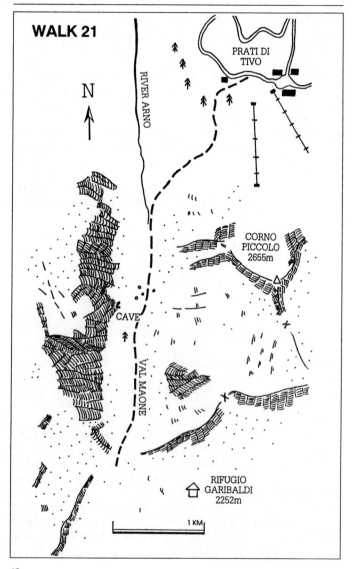

WALK 21

N

RIVER ARNO

PRATI DI TIVO

CORNO
PICCOLO
2655m

CAVE

VAL MAONE

RIFUGIO
GARIBALDI
2252m

1 KM

Route: From the chair-lift station at Prati di Tivo (1465m) walk W along the road for 250m and then go L along an obvious, wide path. This enters some woods where there is a barrier (red/white/red indication) and then on to a clearing at 1520m before descending for 1km to 1435m before a small waterfall (40mins). Here it meets up with a path on the R that comes up the valley from Pietracamela. Stay on the main path S up to a plateau strewn with large boulders (1520m) and then on up to another at 1585m (25mins); two boulders to the R of the path appear to be propping each other up! The path narrows now as it climbs the Val Maone with the rocky buttresses of Pizzo d'Intermesoli on your R and the slopes of the Valle dei Ginepri on your L. After passing through a small wooded area, the path climbs gradually to a terrace (1850m/45mins) where the Val Maone ends just beyond the last of Pizzo d'Intermesoli's buttresses.

22: Rifugio Franchetti (2433m)

Location:	Gran Sasso d'Italia
Grade:	1
Time:	2hrs
Total ascent:	418m
Total distance:	3.5km

Character: Recent renovation of the path up to this refuge has made this an excursion that can be attempted by all walkers. Like the Val Maone itinerary, this is Alpine in character. The path zigzags gradually up to the refuge from where there is a fabulous view of Corno Piccolo's East face and Corno Grande's summits.

Route: Take the chair-lift from Prati di Tivo up to La Madonnina (2015m) and follow the wide path to the L of the Madonna shrine near the chair-lift station. Stay on this gravelly path which goes L at a fork (2060m) and leads to a shoulder (Passo delle Scalette) at 2100m before entering the Vallone delle Cornacchie. Cross an area strewn with boulders (the path actually passes through a natural arch formed by two giant boulders - 2140m) and traverse below a rock wall (new fixed cable here). The path then zigzags gently up to the refuge (2433m/1hr 15mins).

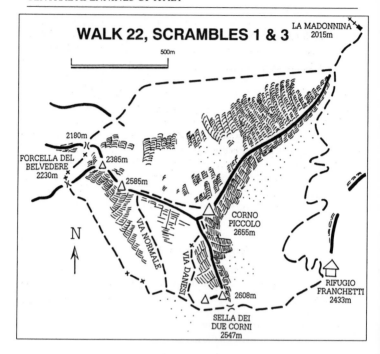

23: Rifugio Duca degli Abruzzi (2388m)

Location:	Gran Sasso d'Italia
Grade:	1
Time:	1hr 15mins
Total ascent:	258m
Total distance:	2km

Character: A short walk to the Portella Ridge which grants a great view of Corno Grande and the Val Maone. The refuge can be seen from Albergo di Campo Imperatore where the walk begins.

Route: From Albergo di Campo Imperatore (2130m), head N passing to the L of the observatory and continue up the slope as the path

WALK 23 & 25

1 KM

MONTE
AQUILA
2495m

SELLA DI
MONTE AQUILA
2335m

RIFUGIO DUCA
DEGLI ABRUZZI
2388m

MONTE PORTELLA
2385m

N

ALBERGO DI
CAMPO IMPERATORE
2130m

zigzags to a fork (2210m). Go L here (sign for refuge) and then R at the next fork (2244m). This path zigzags up to the ridge and the refuge (2388m/45mins).

24: Corno Grande, West Summit (2912m) - Via Normale

Location:	Gran Sasso d'Italia
Grade:	2
Time:	4hrs 45mins
Total ascent:	812m
Total distance:	10km

Character: The highest mountain in the Apennines! This walk involves one steep step up a scree slope to the Sella del Brecciaio (possible snow patches) and a scree path to the summit thereafter.
Route: From Albergo di Campo Imperatore (2130m) take the path

L of the observatory up a steep slope to a fork at 2210m. Go R here (marked "Corno Grande") along the evident path that traverses the slope and then zigzags up to Sella di Monte Aquila (2335m/ 40mins). Follow the ridge R (NE) for 100m to a fork and go L here (marked "Corno Grande - Via Normale") along the path that

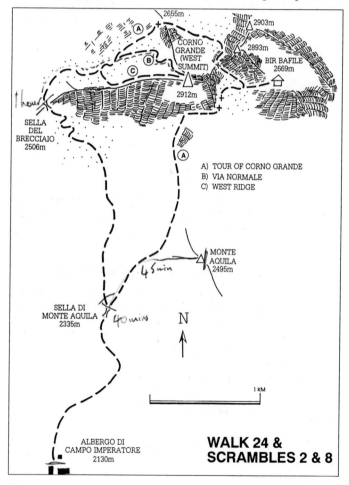

traverses N the entire upper slopes of Campo Pericoli before climbing a steep scree slope to Sella del Brecciaio (2506m/1hr). There is a cemented cairn here indicating the Via ferrata Brizio that goes L. Go straight instead up a path that curves round to the N side of the W ridge of Corno Grande's W summit and then up to a large scree area known as Conca degli Invalidi (2615m). Keep L at the first obvious fork and go R at the second (L for Passo del Cannone and Rifugio Franchetti). Follow this path up the steep slope to a rocky shoulder, then a steep step to the ridge that leads up to the summit (2912m/1hr 15mins).

25: Monte Aquila (2495m)

Location:	Gran Sasso d'Italia (see Map P51)
Grade:	1
Time:	2hrs 30mins
Total ascent:	375m
Total distance:	5km

Character: Easy, panoramic excursion to one of Gran Sasso's less frequented peaks. There is a grand view of Corno Grande's South-East face from the summit as well as the rugged Valle dell'Inferno below.

Route: Reach Sella di Monte Aquila (2335m) on foot from Albergo di Campo Imperatore (see Walk 24: Corno Grande) and continue NE along the ridge, avoiding the path L that traverses N the Campo Pericoli slopes and instead following the ridge faithfully to a grassy shoulder where you go R up a vague path (number 4A - red/yellow painted circle) that climbs the grassy ridge to the summit of Monte Aquila (2495m/45mins from Sella di Monte Aquila).

26: Fondo della Salsa

Location:	Gran Sasso d'Italia
Grade:	1
Time:	2hrs
Total ascent:	410m
Total distance:	4km

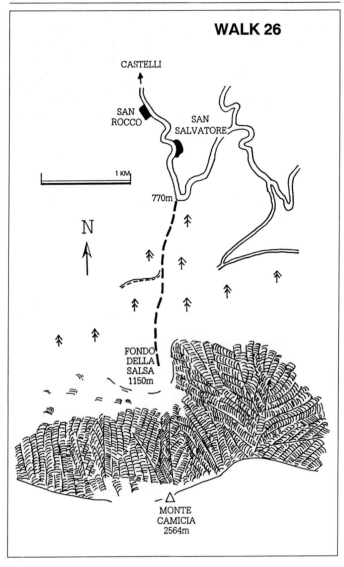

WALK 26

CASTELLI

SAN ROCCO

SAN SALVATORE

1 KM

770m

N

FONDO DELLA SALSA 1150m

MONTE CAMICIA 2564m

Character: A short walk through woods to the base of the gigantic North face of Monte Camicia, dubbed "The Eiger of the Apennines".
Route: Drive S from Castelli village (497m/10km from Isola del Gran Sasso d'Italia) past the houses that make up San Rocco (681m) to those of San Salvatore (740m) and park here. Continue up the road for 400m and at the first bend (770m) there is a path indicated by a yellow sign on the R side of the road with the words "Sentiero dei 4 Vadi" on it. Follow this through the woods to a gap on a rib (857m) where there is quite a good view of Monte Camicia's North face. The path then descends a little before rising again and arriving at a fork (887m). Go L here up through the woods to a clearing and a stream; there is a small pump-house on the L. The view of the North face is extremely good from here. It is possible to continue up alongside the stream to the base of the face, but it is best not to venture too close because of the danger of rockfall (1150m/1hr 15mins).

Scrambles

Prati di Tivo (1465m) - Prati di Tivo village is situated to the north of the Gran Sasso range, about 25km from Montorio al Vomano (SS 80/SW of Teramo).

Albergo di Campo Imperatore (2130m) - Situated to the south of the Gran Sasso range. Either drive up the SS 17 bis road from Fonte Cerreto (27km) or take the cable-car from Fonte Cerreto. The SS 17 bis is often not clear of snow until early summer, so look out for signs at Fonte Cerreto which will indicate if it is possible to drive all the way. Fonte Cerreto (1120m) is 4km from the village of Assergi. Come off the L'Aquila (A 24) motorway at the junction signposted for Assergi, 17km from L'Aquila just before the Gran Sasso tunnel. The words "through route" and "rib" are explained in the Rock Climbs Glossary.

1: Tour of Corno Piccolo - Sentiero Ventricini

Location:	Gran Sasso d'Italia (see Map P50)
Grade:	S I/II
Time:	3hrs 15mins
Total ascent:	approx. 600m

Character: An interesting, panoramic tour that has several "via ferrata" sections just before the final traverse below the North face of Corno Piccolo.

Route: Reach Rifugio Franchetti (2433m) in the Vallone delle Cornacchie (see Walk 22: Rifugio Franchetti) from La Madonnina (2015m) and follow the path up the valley that traverses a slope before zigzagging steeply to Sella dei Due Corni at 2547m (path number 5, red/yellow/red indication). Go R here, descending past the rocky monoliths of Punta dei Due and Campanile Livia on your R to the start of the Via Danesi (number 3D - red/yellow circle). Just below this to the L is a plaque indicating the "Sentiero per Paolo

Ventricini". Continue downhill past this plaque and the start of Corno Piccolo's Via Normale (2400m), following the red circles to a metal cable at 2350m. Cross a gully (possibly filled with snow) and descend to a through route (hole formed by lodged boulder) after which there are more cables and a metal ladder before a slight ascent to a gap. Descend to cross a gully and then ascend to another gap (2335m) where there is a good view of the Prima and Seconda Spalla walls. A gap formed by two obelisks on a rocky rib follows and then a rocky descent to a gully where there are more red paint marks. Climb to a shoulder, then descend before ascending to the Forcella del Belvedere (2230m/1hr 15mins) where there are some old cables rolled up round a rock. From here descend a steep channel (cables and two ladders) to a scree gully (Canale del tesoro nascosto) and go R up this (red marks) for 50m before turning L and using more cables to reach a gap on a ridge. Descend the grassy slopes on the other side (20m) to the path that goes R (E) and is soon marked by metal poles. The path traverses the grassy slopes below the North face of Corno Piccolo and then joins up with the wide path that comes up from the La Madonnina chair-lift station (2060m/45mins).

2: Tour of Corno Grande

Location:	Gran Sasso d'Italia
	(see Map P52)
Grade:	S I/II
Time:	5hrs
Total ascent:	680m

Character: Similar in many ways to the Tour of Corno Piccolo; there are obvious paths up gentle slopes at the beginning followed by "via ferrata" and grade I/II rock sections in the more remote parts of Gran Sasso and finally a simple descent back to the starting point. The rock in the gully and chimney leading to the Forchetta del Calderone is sound, making a very pleasant ascent.
Route: From Albergo di Campo Imperatore (2130m) take the evident path L of the observatory that climbs to a fork at 2210m and go R here (marked "Corno Grande"). A long traverse follows before a

SCRAMBLE 2

SCRAMBLE 2

BIVACCO
BAFILE

S.F.

short zigzag up to the Sella di Monte Aquila (2335m/40mins). Go R here, descending slightly to another fork where you go R again. This path climbs the grassy ridge to a shoulder where path no. 4A departs R for Monte Aquila. Stay on the main path instead (no. 4) which leads to a grassy terrace (Sella di Corno Grande) at 2421m. The path steepens here, zigzagging up past a giant boulder (Il Sassone) at 2570m to a flat area where there is a plaque indicating the start of the Direttissima route beyond (2600m/50mins). Go R here (path no. 4), descending slightly before traversing across two gullies to the base of the SSE ridge of Corno Grande (overhang) where there is a small bivvy cave. A metal ladder and cable follow and then you must climb the slanting rock wall on your L (grade II/ red-yellow-red indication) to reach another cable and a ledge. Then a short traverse (cable) to a gap on a ridge is followed by a long traverse of the scree/snow slopes below the East face of Corno Grande. Continue thereafter in slight ascent to a steep scree gully (40mins). Here you can go R up to the Bafile bivvy hut (2669m/ +15mins) if you wish. Keep L of the steep scree gully, climbing another narrower one marked "no. 4" on sound rock. At about

Scrambles on the Tour of Corno Grande

2700m if the gully is still full of snow, climb L up onto a thin ridge (grade II) and follow this up to where the gully narrows again. If there is still snow to be found here, climb the L side and then traverse at the top to exit by the R wall. A chimney follows this (2750m) leading up to the Forchetta del Calderone (2790m / gap on the Corno Grande / Torrione Cambi ridge). Descend the gully on the other side (15m) and go R (indication) to reach a wide, sloping scree ledge that you must traverse to the far side where there is a gully / ramp that descends beside the North-West face of Corno Grande's central summit. Near the bottom of this, cross an obvious slanting ledge to reach the scree/snow area below the Calderone glacier (2680m / 1hr 15mins). Continue along a boulder rib to the R of the hollow and then a rocky, scree section (red / yellow circle) to a fork below a rock wall (2655m). The descending path R goes to Sella dei Due Corni and Rifugio Franchetti. Instead continue straight here to a small ridge and after this go L up a wall (chain / cable) for 15m and then R up an easy wall (marked No. 5). A long traverse along a scree path takes you to Conca degli Invalidi (2615m / large scree area), passing the turnings L for Corno Grande's Via Normale and W ridge and eventually curving L round to the Sella del Brecciaio (2506m) where there is a cemented cairn. Continue straight here to descend the steep scree slope on the other side of the ridge, before a long traverse of the upper slopes of Campo Pericoli to Sella di Monte Aquila (2335m / 1h 15mins). Descend the path L at the marked fork here to return to Albergo di Campo Imperatore (20mins).

3: Corno Piccolo - South-West Face Via Danesi

Location:	Gran Sasso d'Italia (see Map P50)
Grade:	S I/II
Time:	3hrs 45mins
Total ascent:	640m

Character: A "via ferrata" route on the South-West face of Corno Piccolo that has an interesting through route just before the summit ridge. Splendid panorama from the top on a clear day - the Monti della Laga chain to the west, the Adriatic Sea to the north and Corno Grande to the east.

Route: Reach the start of the Via Danesi (2475m) from La Madonnina (see Walk 22: Rifugio Franchetti and Scramble 1: Tour of Corno Piccolo). This is clearly indicated ("3D" / red-yellow circle). Go up a short gully to a gap and then follow a vague path up the wide scree gully on the other side. Cross over a rocky rib and a gully to begin the diagonal ascent from R to L below Torre Cichetti (monolith), before climbing an evident scree groove on your R and a dièdre where there are metal ladders. After this go L up a gully full of large boulders and take your rucksack off when you reach the red painted triangle below the through route (hole created by lodged boulder) that you will have to squeeze through (or climb rock wall on the L which is grade III). Now go R up a chimney to a gap on the main ridge where there is a great view of the Teramo countryside and the Adriatic coast. Follow the boulder ridge L (summit visible, cross on the top), passing between giant boulders to arrive at a metal cable. Then continue along the ridge to the summit block at the start of which you will find another cable. An easy rock slope then leads to the summit (2655m / 1hr from 2475m).

Descent: Corno Piccolo Via Normale: Descend the easy slabs to the R of the cable (wide W ridge) to 2580m where the ridge flattens out about 40m before the summit of Prima Spalla (2585m) and go L down a narrow gully (red arrow). A path leads down to a through route and then continues traversing to a gap beside an isolated boulder. Descend the scree gully on the other side and go L to climb down a rocky step (10m) to reach the path that now descends diagonally. Climb a 15m rock channel to an easy, mixed grass and rock slope and follow the path down to the Valle dei Ginepri (2410m), ascending L where there are some red circles painted on boulders.

4: Corno Grande, East Summit - Via Normale

Location:	Gran Sasso d'Italia
Grade:	S I/II
Time:	4hrs 15mins
Total ascent:	888m

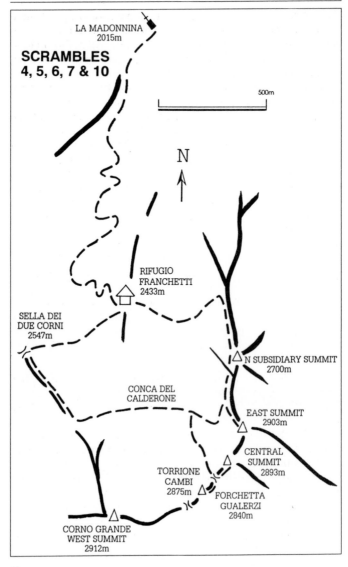

LA MADONNINA
2015m

**SCRAMBLES
4, 5, 6, 7 & 10**

500m

N

RIFUGIO
FRANCHETTI
2433m

SELLA DEI
DUE CORNI
2547m

N SUBSIDIARY SUMMIT
2700m

CONCA DEL
CALDERONE

EAST SUMMIT
2903m

CENTRAL
SUMMIT
2893m

TORRIONE
CAMBI
2875m

FORCHETTA
GUALERZI
2840m

CORNO GRANDE
WEST SUMMIT
2912m

Character: The ascent to the Conca del Calderone is a gentle and panoramic one following evident paths up to the southernmost glacier in Italy, the Ghiacciaio del Calderone. After this a short scramble to one of the highest points in the Apennines, the majestic E summit of Corno Grande.

Route: Reach the Sella dei Due Corni (2547m) from La Madonnina (see Walk 22: Rifugio Franchetti and Scramble 1: Tour of Corno Piccolo) and go L up the wide, scree ridge in the direction of Corno Grande's W summit (indicated "Passo del Cannone"), keeping to the path on the L side of the ridge to a fork below a rock wall (2655m) and go L here across scree (red/yellow circles) to the boulder rib L of the Conca del Calderone (2680m/corrie). Follow path 3C (red/yellow circles) up to the rocky slopes below Corno Grande's E summit and ascend R a little before using the fixed cables to climb straight and then L all the way to the ridge and go R up this to the summit (2903m/50mins from the Conca del Calderone).

5: Corno Grande, East Summit - North Ridge Route

Location:	Gran Sasso d'Italia (see Map P62)
Grade:	S I/II
Time:	4hrs 45mins
Total ascent:	888m

Character: A longer scramble than the Via Normale involving the ascent of a diagonal ledge followed by the long N ridge to Corno Grande's E summit. There are marvellous views of the giant Paretone wall from the ridge.

Route: Reach Rifugio Franchetti (2433m) from La Madonnina (see Walk 22: Rifugio Franchetti) and take the narrow path that begins directly behind the refuge. This traverses a slope to the obvious diagonal ledge that cuts across the face to the North ridge. Follow the steep ledge (fixed cables are not to be trusted though), crossing two gullies before reaching the end of the ledge where you continue diagonally L up easy, sloping walls to the ridge and the N subsidiary peak (2700m/1hr from the refuge). Continue along the ridge up easy rock sections to the summit (2903m / 40mins from N subsidiary summit).

Descent: Return down the N ridge to where the via Normale descends L (fixed cables) to the Conca del Calderone (2680m) and then down to Rifugio Franchetti (2433m).

SCRAMBLE 5

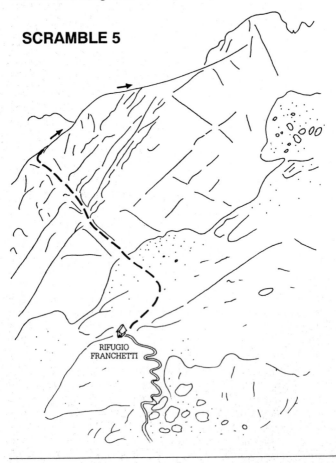

On the path to the Rifugio Franchetti
(East face of Corno Piccolo in the background)

Cascata delle Scalette
Corno Grande, W summit (seen from the Sella di Monte Aquila)

Corno Grande, East summit - North ridge route
(Rifugio Franchetti in the left foreground)

65

6: Corno Grande, Central Summit - Via Gualerzi

Location:	Gran Sasso d'Italia (see Map P62)
Grade:	S I/II
Time:	4hrs 45mins
Total ascent:	958m

Character: The easiest way to reach the Central summit involving some good scrambling in places. It is best not to climb the 160m gully to Forchetta Gualerzi when there are many parties ascending/descending, because of the risk of stonefall.

Route: Reach the Conca del Calderone (2680m) from La Madonnina (see Scramble 4: Corno Grande, E summit, Via Normale) and go up scree slopes to the slanting ledge L of the Cichetti gully that divides Corno Grande's E summit from its central one. Walk up the ledge and then scramble up the gully (marked 3B/red-yellow circle) that climbs diagonally (L to R) below the North-West face of Corno Grande's Central summit to Forchetta Gualerzi (2840m/30mins from Conca del Calderone), the narrow gap between Corno Grande's

West face of Corno Grande Central summit and Torrione Cambi

RNO GRANDE, CENTRAL SUMMIT

SCRAMBLES 6 & 7

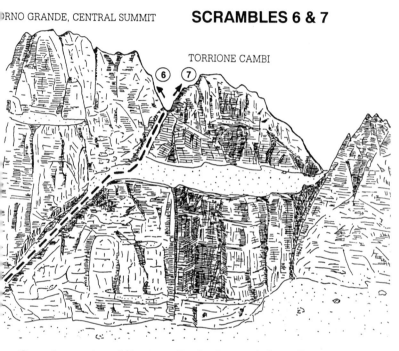

TORRIONE CAMBI

Central summit and Torrione Cambi. Descend the gully on the other side of this gap for 40m where a narrower gully climbs L. Go up this, passing under a boulder lodged in the gully and thereafter exit L climbing easy rock to the summit (2893m/40mins).

7: Torrione Cambi

Location:	Gran Sasso d'Italia (see Map P62)
Grade:	S I/II
Time:	4hrs 15mins
Total ascent:	860m

Character: Same ascent as the preceding scramble to the Forchetta Gualerzi, but easier finish.

Route: Reach Conca del Calderone (2680m) from La Madonnina (see Scramble 4: Corno Grande, E summit, Via Normale) and then ascend the Gualerzi gully (see Scramble 6: Corno Grande, Central summit) to Forchetta Gualerzi (2840m). From this narrow gap climb intuitively R up the ridge to the summit (2875m/15mins from Forchetta Gualerzi).

8: Corno Grande, West Summit - West Ridge

Location:	Gran Sasso d'Italia (see Map P52)
Grade:	S I/II
Time:	5hrs
Total ascent:	812m

Character: Of all the scrambles described in this guidebook, this itinerary involves the least amount of scrambling and is probably the easiest, too, despite the fact that this is the highest mountain in the Apennines. Nevertheless, this route will appeal to those who might prefer a more demanding ascent than the Via Normale and there are certainly some good views from the W ridge.

Route: Reach the Conca degli Invalidi (2615m) from Campo Imperatore (see Walk 24: Corno Grande, W summit, Via Normale) and follow the path R at the first fork that climbs to the W ridge. Go L along this all the way (fixed cable at one point) to the summit (2912m/1hr from Conca degli Invalidi).

Descent: W ridge or Via Normale.

9: Sentiero del Centenario

Location:	Gran Sasso d'Italia)
Grade:	S I/II
Time:	excluding the return walk (see NOTE that follows) 8hrs 45mins. Otherwise 2 days
Total ascent:	1287m

Character: Very long, demanding ridge traverse (12km) above the vast plain of Campo Imperatore. The most interesting (and difficult) section occurs halfway along the ridge between Monte Brancastello (2385m) and Monte Prena (2561m) - this is the scrambling part of the ridge and is approximately 5km long. Towards the end of this traverse there is a vertiginous view of the rocky North face of Monte Camicia that drops straight down to the woods and pastures of Castelli.

NOTE: The 14km return walk along the Campo Imperatore plain can be very tiring, especially on a hot day! The best solution is to leave one car at Fonte Vetica where the Sentiero del Centenario ends and drive to the Vado di Corno track (the starting point) in another, or be dropped off at the starting point and met at Fonte Vetica. Fonte Vetica can be reached by driving 11km E along the SS 17 bis from the Sant' Egidio junction (this junction is 10km E of Albergo di Campo Imperatore) and turning L along an asphalt road for 2km.

Route: From Albergo di Campo Imperatore (2130m) drive 3km E down the SS 17 bis where a track starts L at a bend in the road (1800m). If arriving from Fonte Cerreto (1120m), this track is visible from the SS 17 bis and is approximately 5.5km from the Sant' Egidio junction. Walk up the track to a pass (Vado di Corno) at 1924m and follow the ridge R (E) all the way to the summit of Monte Brancastello (2385m/2hrs). Continue along the ridge, descending to the Vado di Piaverano (2200m/20mins) and ascending to the base of a rock tower (Torri di Casanova) where there is a metal ladder. Descend the other side of the tower using another ladder and then climb

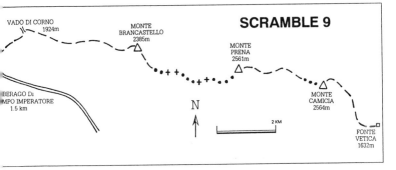

around a second tower by way of a ledge on the R (S) side. Reach the Forchetta di Santa Colomba (2290m / 1hr) by continuing along the undulating ridge and from this gap carry on to a chimney (ladder followed by cables) and a peaklet on the ridge (2469m). Descend loose slabs to a gap and continue along the ridge to a steep slope that leads to an exposed part of the ridge and the summit of Monte Prena (2561m / 1hr 45mins). Now descend to Vado di Ferruccio (2230m / 30mins) and carry on to another gap at 2245m before ascending the ridge to Monte Camicia (2564m) which you reach via a chimney (2hrs). From the summit of Monte Camicia descend R a short, steep slope to a gap on the ridge (2470m) directly above the Vallone di Vradda (SE) and walk down the L side of this valley (path 8A) to Fonte Vetica (1632m) where there is a spring and trattoria (open in summer).

10: Corno Piccolo, North Face

Location:	Gran Sasso d'Italia (see Map P62)
Grade:	S I / II
Time:	4hrs
Total ascent:	787m

Character: Seen from the north, Corno Piccolo looks very much like a giant armchair! The "arms" are strictly reserved for rock climbers, but in between them the rocky terrain is more lenient and as such allows scramblers the chance to reach the summit from this side. There are two possible routes: 1) the Camino di Mezzo gully - a quite direct route to the top that is popular both in summer and winter and which involves some interesting grade II+ passages, and 2) Via Abbate-Acitelli - a much easier scramble which in fact was the route followed by E. Abbate and G. Acitelli during the the first ascent of the peak in 1887.

1) Camino di Mezzo Gully
Route: Take the chair-lift up from Prati di Tivo to La Madonnina (2015m) and then follow the path that keeps L of the Madonna shrine near the chair-lift station as far as a fork at 2060m. Go R here

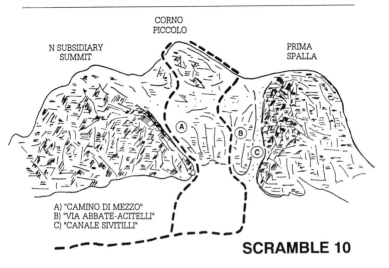

A) "CAMINO DI MEZZO"
B) "VIA ABBATE-ACITELLI"
C) "CANALE SIVITILLI"

SCRAMBLE 10

along a narrow path that traverses the grassy slopes below the North face and which is marked by a number of metal poles. After about 0.5km climb the grassy slopes on your L to reach the R side of the compact face below Corno Piccolo's N subsidiary summit. The Camino di Mezzo gully is the first evident gully to the R of the rocky rib that marks the end of the compact face (see sketch). Climb the gully (rocky arch at the start) to where it forks and go L here to continue on up to the scree area halfway up the face. From here via a channel to the R of a rock rib to gain the NE ridge and then easily to the summit (2655m/2hrs 45mins).

Descent: See Scramble 3: Via Normale descent.

2) Via Abbate-Acitelli

Route: Reach the fork at 2060m mentioned in the approach description to the Camino di Mezzo gully and go R following the narrow path marked by metal poles below the North face of Corno Piccolo. When you are directly below the Canale Sivitilli gully which separates the North face from the rounded Prima Spalla ascend the grassy slopes on your L to the base of the rocky ridge

71

situated to the L of the Canale Sivitilli gully (this gully can be clearly seen from Prati di Tivo - see sketch).

Climb the gully to the L of the rocky ridge to where it forks and go L to reach the scree area halfway up the face. Then continue tending to the R to reach the W ridge which leads easily L up to the summit of Corno Piccolo (2655m/2hrs 45mins).

Descent: See Scramble 3: Via Normale descent.

ROCK CLIMBS

Prati di Tivo (1465m) - Prati di Tivo village is situated to the north of the Gran Sasso range, about 25km from Montorio al Vomano (SS 80/SW of Teramo).

Twenty of the best rock climbs in the Gran Sasso area have been selected for this guidebook and they can all be reached easily from La Madonnina (2015m), the chair-lift station above Prati di Tivo.

Estimate about 45mins/1hr for the approaches to Rock Climbs 6-16 and about 1hr 30mins for the others.

Snow may be encountered in the Canale Bonacossa gully as late as July; it serves as an approach to Rock Climbs 17-20 and descent route for Rock Climbs 14, 15 and 16.

For further information see Rock Climbs in General Information section 1.

Luigi Mario (bottom left) and his family at Ferentillo.
Luigi Mario put up many classic rock routes in Gran Sasso (see Rock Climbs) in the 1950s and 1960s and was the first to bolt sport routes at Ferentillo in 1988

73

ROCK CLIMBS - GLOSSARY

Belay - Anchor point for climbers; a ledge often serves as a good belay point.

Chimney - A wide, vertical fissure in a rock face, often wide enough for a climber to get his/her whole body inside.

Chockstone - A rock or boulder that is lodged in a crack, chimney or gully.

Clessidra - A rock handle with a gap behind it (see General Information section 1).

Crack - Diagonal, horizontal or vertical fissure that you can jam your hands or fingers inside.

Dièdre - A wide groove that often resembles an open book.

Dülfer - A laybacking technique to climb a crack; the climber pulls on the crack edge nearest to him/her while at the same time pushing the feet flat against the other (often protruding) side of the crack.

Flake - A 'leaf' of rock on a face.

Niche - A hollow in a rock face, sometimes below an overhang, that can often serve as a belay point.

Overhang - A shelf of rock that projects over a wall.

Pendulum - Movement across a rock face, sometimes a diagonal descent, to reach a distant crack, chimney, etc.

Pitch - The distance covered by a climber from one belay point to another.

Rib - Generally a small ridge or rocky protuberance on a rock face.

Slab - A slanting rock wall.

Through route - The hole formed by a boulder stuck in a chimney or gully through which a climber/scrambler can pass or squeeze.

1: Via del Tetto

Location:	Campanile Livia, W face.
	Gran Sasso d'Italia
Grade:	D+ (max. V)
Climb time:	1hr 30mins
Total climbing:	105m
First ascent:	A. Bafile and D. Antonelli, 1946

Approach and Description: Campanile Livia is the prominent monolith just beyond Punta dei Due as you look W down the Vallone dei Ginepri from Sella dei Due Corni (2547m). Reach the start of the Via Danesi (see Scramble 1: Tour of Corno Piccolo). There is a large, black roof about 40m above the start of this popular rock climb.

ROCK CLIMBS 1- 20

1st pitch: 25m IV+
Climb a short, grey wall and go L to tackle a dièdre that turns into a narrow chimney. Wide ledge above this.

2nd pitch: 30m V-
Go diagonally R to reach a niche below the black roof and avoid the latter by following a crack R to another ledge.

3rd pitch: 30m V
Go L a few metres in order to climb a 15m wall before following a crack L to a dièdre and go up this to another ledge.

4th pitch: 20m III+
Climb a little to the R for about 10m and then straight on up to the top.

Descent: A short descent E (II+) to the gap between Campanile Livia and Punta dei Due, then R down an easy, rocky channel to the Vallone dei Ginepri slopes or do a 50m double-rope descent to a niche from the new lower-off chain situated just below the summit on the SE face.

Campanile Livia (on the left) and Punta dei Due (on the right)
seen from the south

2: Direttissima dei Teramani

Location:	Campanile Livia, S face.
	Gran Sasso d'Italia (see Map P75)
Grade:	TD (max. VI-)
Climb time:	1hr 45mins
Total climbing:	110m
First ascent:	P. Jannetti and C. Arnoni, 1971

**ROCK CLIMBS
2, 3 & 4**

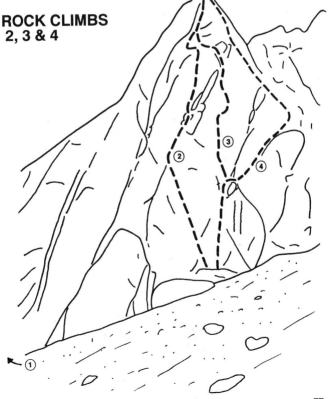

Approach and Description: Reach the base of the South face of Campanile Livia (see Scramble 1: Tour of Corno Piccolo). Direttissima dei Teramani starts just to the R of a giant boulder below the South face, following a dièdre that climbs diagonally L.

1st pitch: 35m VI-

Follow the dièdre to a crack and climb this, tackling a chockstone on its R side before reaching a good belay point.

2nd pitch: 30m VI-

Continue up the crack for about 10m where it forks and follow the L crack to a flake.

3rd pitch: 45m V+

Go L a little before continuing up the crack to a ledge below a yellow wall. Then go L again to climb a slab and after a crack that leads to the ridge and on up to the summit of Campanile Livia.

Descent: See Rock Climb 1.

3: Diretta Consiglio - Mario

Location:	Campanile Livia, S face. Gran Sasso d'Italia (see Map P75, Rock Climb P77)
Grade:	D+ (max. V)
Climb time:	1hr 30mins
Total climbing:	110m
First ascent:	P. Consiglio and L. Mario, 1956

Approach and Description: Reach the base of the South face of Campanile Livia (see Scramble 1: Tour of Corno Piccolo). The route starts up an evident crack to the L of two black, parallel stripes on the R side of the South face.

1st pitch: 20m V

Follow the crack to a ledge.

2nd pitch: 30m V

Climb the slab above L following a thin crack (Dülfer) that includes a tricky horizontal move R (bolt) before continuing up and then L to a niche.

3rd pitch: 20m IV+
Follow the crack above to a ledge situated below an overhanging wall.
4th pitch: 40m IV+
Traverse L to climb a thin crack that leads to the SE ridge and follow this up to the top of Campanile Livia.
Descent: See Rock Climb 1.

4: Via dei Triestini

Location:	Campanile Livia, S to SE face.
	Gran Sasso d'Italia
	(see Map P75, Rock Climb P77)
Grade:	D (max. V)
Climb time:	1hr 30mins
Total climbing:	105m
First ascent:	A. Bafile, G. Del Vecchio and
	P. Zaccaria, 1948

Approach and Description: Reach the base of the South face of Campanile Livia (see Scramble 1: Tour of Corno Piccolo). This route starts up the same crack mentioned in Rock Climb 3.
1st pitch: 20m V
Follow the crack to a ledge.
2nd pitch: 20m IV+
Do not continue up the crack, but instead go diagonally R to reach a good belay stance on the SE ridge.
3rd pitch: 45m IV-
Traverse L a little before climbing up a good line of cracks to a ledge below a slab.
4th pitch: 20m IV
Climb the slab via a crack to reach the top.
Descent: See Rock Climb 1.

5: Via D'Armi - Marsilii

Location:	Punta dei Due, SW face.
	Gran Sasso d'Italia (see Map P75)
Grade:	AD+ (max. IV)
Climb time:	1hr 30mins
Total climbing:	120m
First ascent:	D. D'Armi and B. Marsilii, 1932

Approach and Description: Reach Sella dei Due Corni (2547m) from La Madonnina (see Scramble 1: Tour of Corno Piccolo). There are three long chimneys on the SW face of Punta dei Due and this route follows the one furthest to the R. Descend the scree/grass slope W to the base of the face where there is a boulder situated below several diagonal cracks.

1st pitch: 30m II

Begin to the L of the boulder and climb easy rock to the base of a short dièdre.

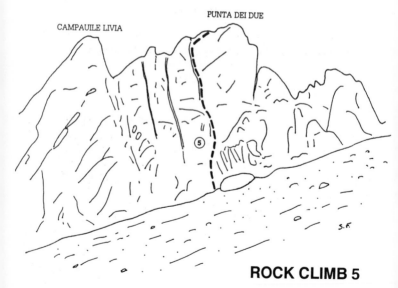

CAMPAUILE LIVIA   PUNTA DEI DUE

ROCK CLIMB 5

2nd pitch: 30m IV
Climb the dièdre and then in the chimney as far as a vertical wall
which affords two cracks.
3rd pitch: 35m IV
Follow the crack on the L, then the one on the R and afterwards
again in the chimney to the ridge.
4th pitch: 25m IV-
Climb slabs on the R to reach the top.
Descent: Go N slightly along the ridge that leads to Corno Piccolo
as far as a gap where you can do a 20m double-rope descent E to a
ledge and go R along this to then descend the South face of Punta dei
Due via a chimney and gully.

6: Ben Hur

Location:	Torre Cichetti, E face.
	Gran Sasso d'Italia (see Map P75)
Grade:	TD (max. VI-)
Climb time:	3hrs
Total climbing:	255m
First ascent:	P. Abbate and A. Monti, 1981

ROCK CLIMB 6

Approach and Description: Just before reaching the Franchetti refuge (see Walk 22: Rifugio Franchetti) cut across the scree/ boulder slopes W to the flat wall situated to the L of an evident cave.

1st pitch: 35m IV, then V

Climb the wall via a crack to a niche (possible belay) below a small overhang and climb up over this to then follow a dièdre to a ledge.

2nd pitch: 35m IV-

Go R across a slab to easier ground and a belay stance beneath a large flake.

3rd pitch: 20m IV-

Climb the flake to reach a ledge below the prominent red roof (this roof is visible from the scree slopes).

4th pitch: 30m VI-

Climb 5m to the crack under the roof and follow this L to a small dièdre where there is a good belay point.

5th pitch: 30m IV

Continue up the dièdre to a niche.

6th pitch: 25m IV+

Climb L side of overhanging block and then traverse L across easy ground.

7th/8th pitches: 80m III

Continue diagonally L (good slabs) to the ridge.

Descent: Reach the Via Danesi on the South face via easy rock slabs/ gullies and reverse this scramble (see Scramble 3: Via Danesi).

7: Via del Monolito

Location:	Il Monolito, East face of Corno Piccolo. Gran Sasso d'Italia (see Map P75)
Grade:	TD- (max. VI)
Climb time:	3hrs
Total climbing:	320m
First ascent:	F. Cravino, L. D'Angelo and S. Jovane, 1956

ROCK CLIMBS 7 & 8

Approach and Description: From La Madonnina (2015m) follow the path that goes to Rifugio Franchetti (see Walk 22: Rifugio Franchetti) and just before reaching the refuge leave the path to walk W across a scree/boulder slope to the base of the aptly named Il Monolito, the monolithic E face of Corno Piccolo. The difficulties

83

begin above the evident ledge that cuts across the face about two-thirds of the way up (see sketch).

Reach the evident ledge by climbing to an obvious rib on the far L side of Il Monolito and then via easy rock (30mins/max III-). Go L now to reach the large slab leaning against the face below a giant roof. Start just beyond the chimney crack formed by the slab and face.

1st pitch: 25m II+
Climb an easy chimney to the base of a crack.

2nd pitch: 40m V
Follow the crack, then dièdre to below an evident triangular-shaped roof and avoid this by going R to a slab belay.

3rd pitch: 40m VI
Follow the crack above, avoiding the top part of this (overhanging) by going R onto the slab wall and up to the belay point.

4th/5th pitches: 60m III
Climb intuitively to the summit now via evident chimneys.

Descent: See Via Normale: Scramble 3.

8: Via Di Federico - De Luca

Location:	Il Monolito, East face of Corno Piccolo. Gran Sasso d'Italia (see Map P75, Rock Climb P83)
Grade:	TD (max. V+)
Climb time:	3hrs
Total climbing:	330m
First ascent:	G. Di Federico and E. De Luca, 1980

Approach and Description: Climb easy rock (III-) to the evident ledge mentioned in Rock Climb 7 and then go L to the chimney crack between the large slab and face situated below the giant roof.

1st pitch: 20m V
Climb the chimney crack to the top of the slab.

2nd pitch: 35m V-

Traverse R across the slab face below the giant roof for approximately 20m before climbing to the R edge of the roof and up round it to a belay below overhangs.

3rd pitch: 25m V+
Go L to tackle a rib and afterwards L again a little to climb a crack and slab to a good belay stance.

4th pitch: 40m V+
Continue up the slab to reach a diagonal (R to L) crack and follow this, climbing over a rib, to another slab section to belay.

5th/6th pitches: 60m III
Climb intuitively to the summit via evident chimneys.

Descent: See Via Normale: Scramble 3.

9: Spigolo a Destra della Crepa

Location:	East face of Corno Piccolo's N subsidiary summit, Gran Sasso d'Italia (see Map P75)
Grade:	TD (max. VI-)
Climb time:	4hrs
Total climbing:	345m
First ascent:	L. Mario and E. Caruso, 1961

Approach and Description: Follow Walk 22: Rifugio Franchetti from La Madonnina (2015m) and just before reaching the refuge go W across the scree slopes to the base of the giant dièdre known as La Crepa which is situated to the R of Il Monolito (see Rock Climb 7). This classic route more or less follows the prominent rib to the R of La Crepa.

1st pitch: 35m V-
Start up the giant dièdre (about 20m) before climbing R (slab section) to a ledge.

2nd pitch: 40m IV
Continue diagonally R and then vertically via easier ground to the edge of the rib.

3rd pitch: 35m V
Follow the rib for about 4m before traversing R a little and then

ROCK CLIMB 9

continuing up to below an overhang. Skirt this going R (smooth slab) up to a mediocre belay stance.

4th pitch: 25m IV

Continue on up to a scree ledge below overhangs and go L along this to the rib's edge.

Spigolo a destra della Crepa (Rock Climb 9)
follows the ridge edge between sun and shadow

87

5th pitch: 20m VI-

Climb an overhanging dièdre L of the rib, then via a wall (straight up then R) to reach two parallel cracks.

6th pitch: 40m VI-

Follow the crack on the L to begin with (the cracks join up) and then continue on up to the top of an evident pillar.

7th pitch: 20m III

Continue on up to a ledge.

8th pitch: 40m V+

Climb the slab above that is situated below some overhangs and go R a little to climb another slab and so reach the rib's edge. From here (protection) a pendulum descent R must be undertaken to reach some cracks which lead to a belay above a boulder.

9th pitch: 45m IV

Climb to a horizontal crack and follow this R (Dülfer) to the bottom of a chimney. Climb this and belay above.

10th pitch: 45m III+

Climb intuitively from here to the N ridge of Corno Piccolo.

Descent: Go L up the ridge to the summit of Corno Piccolo and then descend the Via Normale (see Scramble 3: Via Danesi).

10: Corno Piccolo - North-East Ridge

Location:	Gran Sasso d'Italia (see Map P75)
Grade:	AD- (max. III+)
Climb time:	3hrs 30mins
Total climbing:	325m
First ascent:	E. Jannetta and A. Bonacossa, 1923

Approach and Description: From La Madonnina (2015m) follow the path that goes to Rifugio Franchetti (see Walk 22) for approx. 5mins before leaving it to climb the grassy slopes that are, in effect, the tail ends of Corno Piccolo's NE ridge. Upon reaching the first rocky section of the ridge, go L to reach a grassy ledge that overlooks the Vallone delle Cornacchie (E).

1st pitch: 50m III+

Climb the dièdre situated to the L of the ridge. This turns into a narrow chimney which leads up to a good belay ledge.

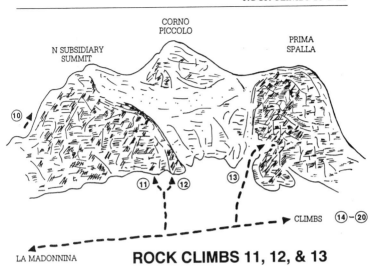

ROCK CLIMBS 11, 12, & 13

2nd pitch: 45m III

Climb another chimney just to the R of the ridge followed by a dièdre and short slab section to reach another good belay ledge. Continue easily up the ridge (max. II), keeping a little to the R of it when you reach the final summit slabs.

Descent: See Via Normale: Scramble 3.

11: Via Bachetti - Calibani

Location:	Corno Piccolo, N face. Gran Sasso d'Italia (see Map P75, Rock Climb above)
Grade:	D- (max. IV+)
Climb time:	2hrs
Total climbing:	135m
First ascent:	F. Bachetti and M. Calibani, 1968

Approach and Description: The North face of Corno Piccolo dominates the grassy slopes above Prati di Tivo. Upon reaching La Madonnina chair-lift station (2015m) follow the path past the

Madonna shrine and go R at a fork (2060m). A narrow path traverses the grassy slopes below the North face and is marked by a number of metal poles. From the fork follow the path for about 0.5km and then climb the grassy slopes L to reach the R side of the compact face below Corno Piccolo's N subsidiary summit (see sketch). The Via Bachetti-Calibani climbs the dièdre to the L of a slab wall that has an evident, arching crack on its lower section. The dièdre to the R of this slab instead is that mentioned in Rock Climb 12 after which comes the final rock rib on this part of the N face. Reach a ramp below the slab wall that leads up to two prominent, vertical cracks.

1st pitch: 25m IV+

Climb the short ramp and then the L crack to a belay stance.

2nd pitch: 40m IV+

Continue up the crack/dièdre (L at a fork) to a ledge on the R.

3rd pitch: 25m IV

Again up the dièdre to reach the base of an overhang.

4th pitch: 45m IV

Go L to reach a slab with an evident crack and climb this (overhang at the end) and a compact slab above to easier ground. Now either continue up easy gullies/rock ribs to the summit of Corno Piccolo after which you can descend the Via Normale (see Scramble 3) or descend the Camino di Mezzo gully on your R.

12: Via Iskra

Location:	Corno Piccolo, North face. Gran Sasso d'Italia (see Map P75, Rock Climb P89)
Grade:	D- (max. V-)
Climb time:	2hrs
Total climbing:	155m
First ascent:	F. Cravino and R. Tonini, 1966

Approach and Description: See Rock Climb 11 - This route starts up the dièdre to the L of the final rock rib mentioned in Rock Climb 11 and is approx. 30m R of Via Bachetti-Calibani.

1st pitch: 35m III+

Climb the dièdre to a good belay point.

"Via Iskra" (D-/ V-), Gran Sasso D'Italia

2nd pitch: 40m IV+
Continue up the dièdre to a reasonable belay.
3rd pitch: 40m IV+
Continue up the dièdre L to a ledge below a slab (clessidra above)
and climb this or up the crack R to reach a very good belay ledge R.
4th pitch: 40m V-
Return L to reach a crack (overhang) followed by a traverse L below
a large flake to slabs (cemented U bolt). From here climb the easy
ridge beyond and either continue on up to the summit of Corno
Piccolo via easy gullies / rock ribs and descend the Via Normale (see
Scramble 3) or descend the Camino di Mezzo gully on your R.

13: Via Attenti alle Clessidre

Location:	Prima Spalla, North-East face. Gran Sasso d'Italia (see Map P75,Rock Climb P89)
Grade:	D- (max. IV)
Climb time:	2hrs 30mins
Total climbing:	200m
First ascent:	F. Antonioli, F. Colesanti and D. Mantoan, 1982

Approach and Description: From La Madonnina (2015m) follow the wide path that goes past the Madonna shrine and leads to a fork at 2060m. Go R here and follow the narrow path that traverses the grassy slopes below the North face of Corno Piccolo until you are directly below the Canale Sivitilli gully that separates the North face of Corno Piccolo from the rounded Prima Spalla. This gully is visible from Prati di Tivo (see sketch). Ascend the grassy slopes to reach the bottom of the gully and then climb about 50m up the gully to reach a ledge on the R, below the North-East face of Prima Spalla.

1st pitch: 45m III

Climb the slab above (clessidre) to a reasonable belay.

2nd pitch: 35m IV

Climb to a ledge and then up the slab above briefly before snaking first of all to the R and then to the L to reach a clessidra belay.

3rd pitch: 40m IV

Traverse a couple of metres L before climbing the slab above to a ledge.

4th/5th pitches: 80m IV, then III

Climb a short dièdre on the L followed by a slab section (more clessidre) which gradually relents.

Descent: From the top of Prima Spalla follow the ridge E briefly (the ridge leads to the summit of Corno Piccolo) before descending the Via Normale on your R (see Scramble 3).

14: Via Morandi - Consiglio - De Ritis

Location:	Seconda Spalla, North face.
	Gran Sasso d'Italia (see Map P75)
Grade:	AD (max. IV-)
Climb time:	2hrs 30mins
Total climbing:	230m
First ascent:	B. Morandi, P. Consiglio and
	F. De Ritis, 1956

Approach and Description: Follow the narrow path that traverses the grassy slopes below Corno Piccolo's North face (see Rock Climb 13) and continue past the rounded Prima Spalla's North face to reach the grassy slope directly below the triangular-shaped Seconda Spalla (approx. 1km from the fork at 2060m). This popular route begins up a grassy gully to the R of an evident boulder situated in front of Seconda Spalla's North face.

ROCK CLIMB 14

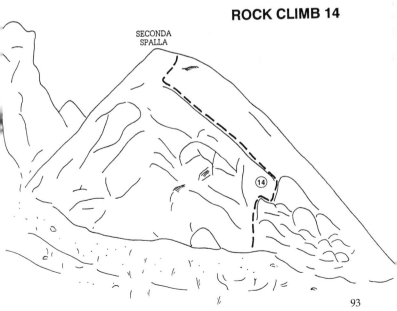

1st pitch: 40m III
Climb the grassy gully (mostly I / II) to reach a scree ledge below an overhang.
2nd pitch: 35m III+
Traverse R to a wide gully and climb this to reach the bottom of a narrow chimney.
3rd pitch: 40m IV-
Climb the chimney to a gap near a large, boulder.
4th pitch: 25m III
Climb the wall to the R of the gap to reach the wide, slanting (L to R) ledge.
5th pitch: 40m III
Follow the ledge for approx. 20m before tackling a rib to reach a ledge.
6th pitch: 50m III+
Climb the slab above and go R of a rocky projection to reach the gentle ridge that leads to the top of Seconda Spalla.
Descent: Reach the gap that separates Seconda Spalla from the higher Prima Spalla and go L down the Canale Bonacossa gully to the narrow path again.

15: Via Mario - Di Filippo

Location:	Seconda Spalla, West face.
	Gran Sasso d'Italia (see Map P75)
Grade:	TD (max. VI)
Climb time:	3hrs 30mins
Total climbing:	300m
First ascent:	L. Mario and F. Di Filippo, 1962

Approach and Description: Follow the Tour of Corno Piccolo (see Scramble 1) in an *anti-clockwise direction,* passing below the North faces of Prima Spalla and Seconda Spalla, then descending the Canale del tesoro nascosto gully and climbing the two ladders that follow. Via Mario - Di Filippo starts up the dièdre that is situated directly above the second ladder.

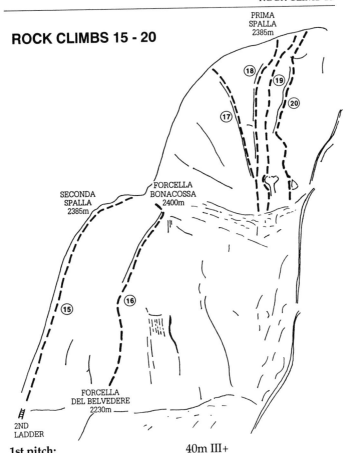

ROCK CLIMBS 15 - 20

PRIMA
SPALLA
2385m

(18)

(19)

(20)

(17)

SECONDA
SPALLA
2385m

FORCELLA
BONACOSSA
2400m

(15)

(16)

FORCELLA
DEL BELVEDERE
2230m

2ND
LADDER

1st pitch: 40m III+
Climb the evident dièdre to a belay stance.

2nd pitch: 35m VI
Continue up the dièdre (thin crack) to below some overhangs and
skirt these by going L (Dülfer) and afterwards up a slab to a ledge.

3rd pitch: 40m V
There are two parallel cracks visible above; climb a short wall to
reach the R crack and follow this for about 20m before traversing L

across the slab to reach the L crack and belay point.

4th pitch: 35m V-

Tackle another short wall to the R to climb a dièdre followed by easier ground and a rock rib. Now continue intuitively for 4 pitches to the top of Seconda Spalla (mostly II+).

Descent: See Rock Climb 14.

16: Via Marsilii - Sivitilli

Location:	Seconda Spalla, South-West face. Gran Sasso d'Italia (see Map P75, Rock Climb P95)
Grade:	AD (max. IV+)
Climb time:	2hrs
Total climbing:	220m
First ascent:	B. Marsilii, E. Sivitilli, O. Trinetti, A. Giancola and V. Franchi, 1930

Approach and Description: See Rock Climb 15 and from the top of the second ladder continue on up to the Forcella del Belvedere (2230m/old cables rolled up round a rock). There are two short chimneys above the Forcella del Belvedere.

1st/2nd pitches: 80m III

Follow the chimney on the L and then up the crack that comes after.

3rd/4th pitches: 60m III-

Continue up a gully that gets steeper before arriving below a chockstone.

5th pitch: 15m IV

Go R under this and up a slab to a rocky projection.

6th pitch: 20m IV+

Climb the smooth slab above and then a chimney (chockstone) that leads up to the ridge. From here climb easily to the top of Seconda Spalla.

Descent: See Rock Climb 14.

Corno Grande (on the left) and Corno Piccolo, Gran Sasso d'Italia
The path that leads to the Tour of Corno Grande scramble (Corno
Grande, W summit in the background) - Scramble 2)

N face of Monte Bove Sud

Climbing the Canalone Chiaretti - Pietrostefani on the North-East face of Monte Terminillo

17: Via Federici - Antonelli

Location:	Prima Spalla, South face.
	Gran Sasso d'Italia
	(see Map P75, Rock Climb P95)
Grade:	D- (max. IV+)
Climb time:	2hrs
Total climbing:	200m
First ascent:	D. Antonelli and F. Federici, 1939

Approach and Description: Reach the base of the North face of Seconda Spalla (see Rock Climb 14) and go L to the Canale Bonacossa gully that separates Seconda Spalla from Prima Spalla. Ascend the gully (grade F+) to a gap at the top (Forcella Bonacossa) at 2400m; the summit of Seconda Spalla is on your R. Reach the scree ledge that skirts the base of the South face of Prima Spalla and follow this until you are directly below the evident cracks that form a V shape. This route follow the L crack and Rock Climb 18 follows the R one.

South Face of Prima Spalla (Corno Piccolo)
seen from the Sentiero Ventricini. Rock Climbs 17 - 20
start from the ledge that is visible in the central area

97

1st pitch: 50m IV-

Climb intuitively to a ledge where the two cracks branch off in different directions.

2nd pitch: 40m IV-

Traverse the slab L to reach the L crack and climb this to where it narrows.

3rd pitch: 40m IV+

The first step of this pitch is the hardest part of the route; a less demanding scree channel follows.

4th/5th pitches: 70m III+

Continue on up to a series of sound slabs which lead to the ridge. Then easily to the summit.

Descent: Via Normale of Corno Piccolo - see Rock Climb 13.

18: Via Mario - Di Filippo

Location:	Prima Spalla, South face.
	Gran Sasso d'Italia
	(see Map P75, Rock Climb P95)
Grade:	TD- (max. V+)
Climb time:	2hrs 30mins
Total climbing:	190m
First ascent:	L. Mario and F. Di Filippo, 1962

Approach and Description: See Rock Climb 17 for approach. There are two distinct cracks that cut right up the middle of the South face and this excellent route follows the R one.

1st pitch: See Rock Climb 17.

2nd pitch: 20m V

Follow the R (vertical) crack to a ledge.

3rd pitch: 35m V+

Continue up the crack to where it forks.

4th pitch: 45m V

Keep R here following the crack to a reasonable belay.

5th pitch: 40m IV+

Go L across a slab to reach a short, thin crack and continue on up to the top of Prima Spalla.

Descent: Via Normale of Corno Piccolo - see Rock Climb 13.

"Val Mario - Di Filippo" (TD/VI), Gran Sasso d'Italia

19: Via Aficionados

Location:	Prima Spalla, South face.
	Gran Sasso d'Italia
	(see Map P75, Rock Climb P95)
Grade:	ED- (max. VII-)
Climb time:	3hrs
Total climbing:	185m
First ascent:	L. Bucciarelli and C. Delisi, 1985

Approach and Description: See Rock Climb 17 for approach. This route is situated to the R of Rock Climbs 17 and 18. It follows a crack on the L side of a large flake after 30m. There are clessidre or bolt-protected belay points and the difficult 3rd pitch is also protected with some bolts.

1st pitch: 30m III+

Climb a narrow chimney to reach the crack that curves to the L.

2nd pitch: 30m VI-

Dülfer the crack (vertical at the start) to reach the top of the large flake that is visible from the bottom of the face.

3rd pitch: 35m VI to VII-
Climb the slab above (long, dark stripes on the rock) following bolts.

4th pitch: 35m VI+
Climb up over a small overhang and then traverse L about 8m to reach a run of cracks that leads to a belay.

5th pitch: 35m V+
Again via the cracks to the point where they fizzle out and shortly after go L a little to climb a slab pillar to a ledge.

6th pitch: 20m IV-
Now go R to climb a dièdre and then on up to the summit.

Descent: Via Normale of Corno Piccolo (see Rock Climb 13).

20: Via Stefano Triboli

Location:	Prima Spalla, South face.
	Gran Sasso d'Italia
	(see Map P75, Rock Climb P95)
Grade:	TD+ (max. VI+)
Climb time:	3hrs
Total climbing:	205m
First ascent:	B. Aldinio, P. Bini and G. Picone, 1978

Approach and Description: See Rock Climb 17 for approach. Via Stefano Triboli starts to the R of Rock Climbs 17, 18 and 19 and climbs the L side of a triangular-shaped flake near the beginning of the route. Later on it follows a prominent crack for two pitches.

1st pitch: 30m V-
Climb slabs and then follow the crack on the L side of the large flake to reach the top of it.

2nd pitch: 20m IV
Go diagonally L to a good clessidra belay.

3rd pitch: 40m VI+
Climb directly up a slab and then a slight dièdre before traversing L and climbing about 10m up to the base of the long, prominent crack.

4th/5th pitches: 75m VI then V+
Climb about 40m up the crack to a clessidra belay and then another
35m up the crack to reach the base of a small overhang.
6th pitch: 40m V+
Tackle the overhang by way of a wide crack to then continue via
slabs to the top.
Descent: Via Normale of Corno Piccolo (see Rock Climb 13).

"Via Colpo Grosso" (ED-/VII-), Gran Sasso d'Italia. (not described)

WINTER CLIMBS

Casali (Marche) - 5km E of Ussita, 10km E of Visso.

Frontignano (Marche) - 9km S of Ussita.

Forca di Presta (Marche / Umbria boundary) - 12km NW of Arquata del Tronto, 8km SE of Castelluccio.

Foce (Marche) - 10km W of Montemonaco.

Balzo (Marche) - 13km N of Arquata del Tronto.

Terminillo - Pian de Valli (Lazio) - 21km NE of Rieti.

Albergo di Campo Imperatore (Abruzzo) - take the cable-car from Fonte Cerreto village near Assergi. Reach Fonte Cerreto by leaving the A 24 motorway at the Assergi junction, 17km from L'Aquila.

Prati di Tivo (Abruzzo) - 6km S of Pietracamela, 25km SW of Montorio al Vomano (Teramo).

1: Monte Bove Nord (Canalone Nord)

Location:	Monti Sibillini
Grade:	PD
Approach ascent:	320m
Climbing:	700m
Character:	Snow to 45°. The snow is nearly always firm and crunchy since the gully sees very little sun.

Approach: From Casali (1080m) follow Walk 6: Val di Panico to where the track zigzags up towards the spring (Sorgenti di Panico / 1285m) and go R past a hut with a steep sloping roof into the woods that hug the base of the North and East faces of Monte Bove Nord. Upon entering the woods go L up through the trees to the bottom of the gully that sweeps down beside the East face of Monte Bove Nord (1hr 30mins).

Description: Climb the gully to its end, but if there are cornices at

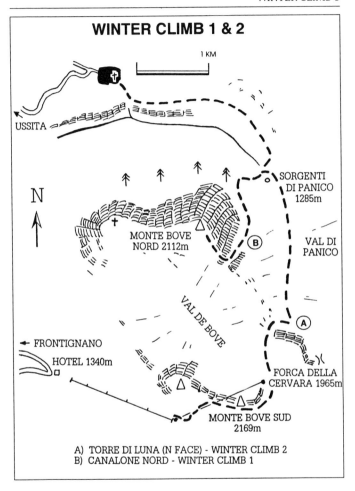

WINTER CLIMB 1 & 2

1 KM

N

USSITA

SORGENTI
DI PANICO
1285m

VAL DI
PANICO

MONTE BOVE
NORD 2112m

B

VAL DE BOVE

A

← FRONTIGNANO

HOTEL 1340m

FORCA DELLA
CERVARA 1965m

MONTE BOVE SUD
2169m

A) TORRE DI LUNA (N FACE) - WINTER CLIMB 2
B) CANALONE NORD - WINTER CLIMB 1

the top then go R before the last rocky outcrop on the R side of the gully and ascend a narrow channel up to the ridge. Go R after this to the summit (2122m/2hrs 15mins).

Descent: From the summit return down the ridge of ascent (SE) past the exit of the gully and continue along the ridge for 1km where you descend a gully on your L (40°) to reach the corrie at the head of the Val di Panico. Descend the valley without difficulties to the spring at 1285m and return to Casali along the track that skirts the N side of the valley (2hrs).

2: Val di Panico (Torre di Luna, North Face)

Location:	Monti Sibillini (see Map p103)
Grade:	TD
Approach ascent:	369m from Frontignano
	chair-lift or 760m from Casali
Climbing:	150m/200m
Character:	Ice to 80°.

Approach: 1) From Frontignano - Go up the track to the R of the Hotel Felicita to the ticket office and take the chair-lift just beyond this to the top station at 1800m. Walk up the slope, keeping to the L of the ski-lift above the top station, for 100m before turning L and going up another slope to a col (2020m) on the Monte Bicco/Bove Sud ridge where there is a cable-car pylon. Follow the ridge R (beware of cornices!) all the way to the summit of Monte Bove Sud

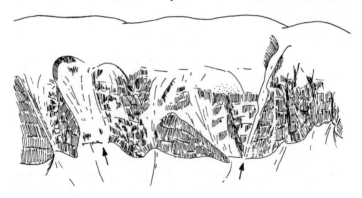

WINTER CLIMB 2

Climbing the first ice wall (80°) on the North face of Torre di Luna, Val di Panico

(2169m/1hr 15mins) and then go NE along the ridge to the top cable-car station (rarely in operation). Descend the gentle, wide ridge N and when the Torre di Luna wall at the head of the Val di Panico comes into view on your R (E) descend a steep gully to reach the base of the wall (1840m/1hr 45mins from the chair-lift station). This approach is less tiring than:
2) From Casali (1080m) - From the parking area in front of Casali church, take the obvious track that passes by the church and which skirts the N side of the valley for 3km to the Sorgente di Panico spring (1285m). Then follow the path that climbs the upper part of the valley to a terrace below a prominent rocky buttress (1550m/

2hrs). Gentle slopes to the R of the buttress lead up to the evident Torre di Luna wall at the end of the Val di Panico (1840m/2hrs 45mins from Casali).

Description: Looking at the wall from the Val di Panico (see Sketch p104), there are two principal gullies: The one on the L is wider and has some large icicle formations. At the very beginning of this gully there is an ice wall (8m/80°) that is best climbed on its R side. An easier section follows this (10m) and the angle then increases (50°/ 60°) before arriving at a second ice wall that is situated on the R side of the gully. Climb this (10m, 70°/80°) to the gentle snow slopes above or, if this ice wall is not in condition, avoid it by veering L below a curtain of icicles and passing a small, isolated tree to the upper slopes. Having reached the wide ridge above, follow it SW towards the Bove Sud cable-car station. If returning to Casali village, descend the gully mentioned in the Frontignano approach to the Val di Panico.

The gully to the R also has an icy start (20m/70°) and this is followed by a narrow channel (20m, 50°/60°) that gradually widens. The angle decreases here and soon after an easy slope then leads up to the ridge. Follow this SW to the Bove Sud cable-car station and the Bove Sud ridge back to the chair-lift station (45mins) or, if returning to Casali, descend the gully mentioned in the Frontignano approach to the Val di Panico (1hr 40mins).

3: Monte Bicco, North Face

Location:	Monti Sibillini
Grade:	AD to D+
Approach ascent:	50m
Climbing:	200m
Character:	Snow gullies and slopes interrupted by horizontal rocky (often icy) steps.

Approach and Description: From the Frontignano top chair-lift station (see Winter Climb 2) go N across a snow gully to reach the path that traverses the slope to a gap on the NW ridge of Monte Bicco and continue R from here to arrive at the base of the North face

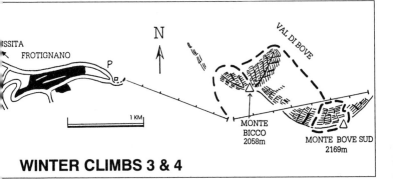

WINTER CLIMBS 3 & 4

(20mins). There is no definite line to follow. Climb intuitively up the slopes, overcoming rocky steps occasionally. Generally, the R side of the face is easier. Depending on the snow conditions, the difficulties encountered can vary from grade AD to D+.

Descent: From the summit (2052m) descend the SE ridge to a col (2020m) where there is a cable-car pylon and go R down the snow slope towards the ski-lift and from there to the chair-lift station (25mins).

4: Monte Bove Sud (North Face)

Location:	Monti Sibillini (see Map above)
Grade:	AD
Approach ascent:	280m
Climbing:	150m
Character:	Snow to 55°and some mixed ground.

Approach: Reach the base of the North face of Monte Bicco (see Winter Climb 3) and continue traversing E below it, descending to skirt the NE ridge near some boulders. Ascend the Val di Bove SW from here to the corrie below the rocky North face of Monte Bove Sud (1900m/50mins).

Description: There is a choice of two gullies (see sketch) and both are grade AD when they are in good condition; otherwise, they can present icy steps that merit a D grading. The lower part of the gully

107

ROCK CLIMB 4

on the L (Canalino Primavera) climbs diagonally R behind a wall (snow to 45°) to an icy/rocky step (piton to the L). After this the gully continues diagonally L up to the summit ridge (max. 50°). Go R from here to the summit (2169m/1hr 15mins).

The gully on the R (Canalino Nord) has a snowy/icy "staircase" start (55°) and then forks, offering you the choice of two snow channels to the Bove Sud/Bicco ridge.

Descent: Descend the ridge W towards Monte Bicco (keep to the L of the ridge - cornices!) and, reaching a cable-car pylon at a col (2020m), go L down an easy snow slope to a ski-lift and descend R to the chair-lift station (30mins).

5: Pizzo del Diavolo (East Face)

Location:	Monti Sibillini
Grade:	AD
Approach ascent:	706m from Forca di Presta
	or 1105m from Foce
Climbing:	360m
Character:	Snow to 60°and some mixed ground.

NOTE: There is a bivvy cave at the base of the NE buttress of Pizzo del Diavolo.

Approach: Reach Rifugio Zilioli from Forca di Presta (see Walk 14:

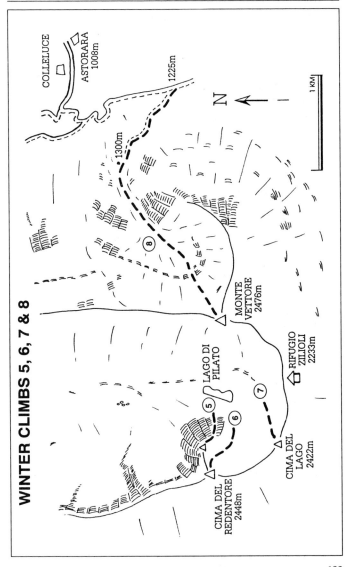

WINTER CLIMBS 5, 6, 7 & 8

COLLELUCE

ASTORARA
1008m

1225m

1300m

N

1 KM

MONTE
VETTORE
2476m

RIFUGIO
ZILIOLI
2233m

LAGO DI
PILATO

⑧

⑤

⑥

⑦

CIMA DEL
REDENTORE
2448m

CIMA DEL
LAGO
2422m

Monte Vettore) and descend N from Sella delle Ciaule (2240m) into the corrie at the head of the Valle del Lago di Pilato and go to the L side of the lake (Lago di Pilato) just below the evident gully on the L side of Pizzo del Diavolo's East face (20mins from Sella delle Ciaule). If you start from Foce village, follow Walk 13: Valle del Lago di Pilato to the lake and go R around it to reach the snow slope below the gully (3hrs 40mins from Foce).

Description: Climb the gully (60°) for 150m to its end and go R across some mixed ground to reach another narrower gully. This leads straight up to the PD snow slope described in Winter Climb 6, but instead of going directly to this turn R up another narrow gully that leads to the summit of Pizzo del Diavolo (2hrs 30mins).

Descent: Go W along the ridge that leads up to Cima del Redentore and before reaching this go L down a wide gully (max. 45°) to the lake in the Lago di Pilato corrie (30mins).

6: Cima del Redentore (South-East Face)

Location:	Monti Sibillini (see Map P109)
Grade:	PD
Approach ascent:	706m from Forca di Presta
	or 1105m from Foce
Climbing:	400m
Character:	Snow to 45°.

NOTE: There is a bivvy cave at the base of the NE buttress of Pizzo del Diavolo.

Approach: See Winter Climb 5.

Description: From the lake (1940m) ascend the snow slopes SW going around the final rocky buttress of Pizzo del Diavolo and then up the wide gully to the ridge that runs down from Cima del Redentore to Pizzo del Diavolo. Go L along the ridge to the summit of Cima del Redentore (2448m/1hr 30mins).

7: Cima del Lago (North Face)

Location:	Monti Sibillini (see Map P109)
Grade:	D-
Approach ascent:	800m from Forca di Presta or 1227m from Foce
Climbing:	250m
Character:	Snow to 50°, some ice.

NOTE: There is a bivvy cave at the base of the NE buttress of Pizzo del Diavolo.

Approach: See Winter Climb 5.
Description: From the lake (1940m) ascend the snow slopes SW towards the triangular North face of Cima del Lago. The gully is the furthest to the L that cuts diagonally up the face to the summit. The start is the hardest part: an 8m tongue of ice (65°) is followed by a snow channel that climbs R to the ridge and then the summit (max. 50°).
Descent: Descend the E ridge of Cima del Lago to Rifugio Zilioli (2233m) and go either L down to the lake and Foce or R for Forca di Presta.

8: Monte Vettore (North-East Face)

Location:	Monti Sibillini (see Map P109)
Grade:	PD+
Approach ascent:	75m. But if the track from Colleluce village is blocked by snow, approx. 275m
Climbing:	1176m
Character:	Snow to 50°.

Approach: From the village of Balzo (886m) drive W through the hamlets of Collefrata, Astorara and Colleluce and just after Colleluce turn L at a junction. The road becomes a track. Go L at the next

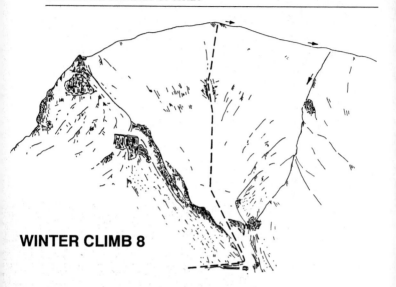

WINTER CLIMB 8

junction, passing a spring on the R after only 20m and continue for 1.5km through a wood and past another spring to a junction (1225m). Park here and walk along the track R that climbs gently for approx. 1.5km to two gates and a fork (1300m). The path R descends to a pump-house. Instead go L to reach the snow gully.

Description: Climb the gully to where a rocky spur divides it in two and go L up a snow slope to a large terrace (1700m) after which the gully fans out like a great funnel. An evident, narrow gully with rocky sides is situated halfway up the face directly below the summit. Climb this (max. 50°) to reach the summit (3hrs 30mins).

Descent: Walk about 700m down the N ridge to the N edge of the great funnel and descend the snow slopes R and a gully to reach the large terrace at 1700m. Descend from here via the route of ascent.

'Workshop' (6b) at Il Balcone, Ferentillo.
Monterivoso village in the background

Climber on Circe (5+) at Ferentillo
Luigi Mario climbing Passeggiando sul nero (7a+) at Ferentillo, at the age of 57!
Mario put up many hard rock routes in the 1950s and 1960s in Gran Sasso and
played a major role in the development of Ferentillo as a sport climbing venue

9: Monte Terminillo (North-East Face) Canalone Chiaretti - Pietrostefani

Location:	Monti Reatini
Grade:	PD+ / AD-
Approach ascent:	140m
Climbing:	260m
Character:	Snow to 45°, one 60° chimney and some mixed ground.

Approach: Drive 1km SE from Terminillo (Pian de Valli / 1614m) to a large parking area opposite some ski-hire shops (1675m) and go L here along an asphalt road that passes a chair-lift (1672m) and skirts the base of the South face of Monte Terminillo before zigzagging up to Rifugio Sebastiani (1820m). This refuge is open throughout

WINTER CLIMB 9

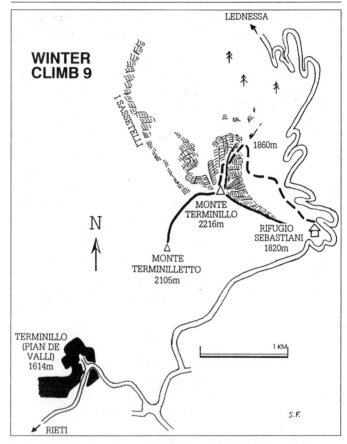

LEDNESSA

WINTER CLIMB 9

I SASSETELLI

1860m

N

MONTE TERMINILLO 2216m

RIFUGIO SEBASTIANI 1820m

MONTE TERMINILLETTO 2105m

TERMINILLO (PIAN DE VALLI) 1614m

1 KM

S.F.

RIETI

the year. From the refuge walk NW up the snow slopes to the L of the road (blocked by snow) to Sella di Leonessa (1901m/20mins) and from this pass go L across slopes towards the East face of Monte Terminillo, in particular two prominent gullies that climb to the summit.

These gullies are both 35°/40° and see more ski-mountaineers than alpinists. Just before reaching these go R traversing the slope below the East face to a rib (1960m/25mins) beyond which there is

114

a drop to the wooded Vallonina. The Canalone Chiaretti - Pietrostefani gully on the North-East face can be seen from this rib on your L (see sketch).

Description: Descend the steep snow slope on the other side of the rib (10m) before traversing L to the bottom of the gully. About 6m after where this starts to narrow and becomes a corridor (1990m) look for two pitons low down on the L wall (1m apart). Continue up the gully to another belay point (35m/piton on a slanting ledge on R wall) and then on up to the third one at 2055m (piton low down on L wall). There is another belay point on the R wall (piton) after 30m just below a chimney to the R of a rocky spur in the gully. Climb this chimney (10m/max. 60°/often icy) to a rock pinnacle on the L that can serve as a running belay. Then an easy 20m slope leads to the ridge and a rocky projection to the L. Climb a steep snow channel to the L of the rocky projection to a gap and then go diagonally R up an icy patch to exit onto the other side of the rocky projection and a col. A mixed step up to the final ridge which leads directly to the summit where there is an iron pillar and a diary in a metal box (2216m/2hrs from the bottom of the gully).

Descent: Either descend the gully on the East face directly below the summit or the SE ridge that leads straight down to the refuge (45mins).

10: Corno Grande W Summit (South Face), Direttissima

Location:	Gran Sasso d'Italia
Grade:	PD
Approach ascent:	470m
Climbing:	300m
Character:	Snow to 45°. A popular winter climb to the summit of the highest peak in the Apennines.

NOTE: If the slopes above Albergo di Campo Imperatore (2130m) have a lot of snow on them, then it would be better to ascend directly to the Duca degli Abruzzi refuge (see Walk 23) and then descend the

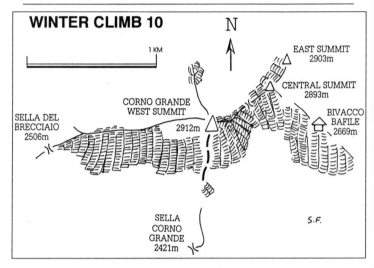

ridge E to Sella di Monte Aquila (2335m) rather than take the path marked "Corno Grande" that traverses the slope to Sella di Monte Aquila described in Scramble 2: Tour of Corno Grande.

Approach: Reach the fork at 2600m where there is a plaque indicating the start of the Direttissima to the L (see Scramble 2: Tour of Corno Grande). The path R (no.4) goes to the Bafile bivouac hut.

Description: Climb the gully to the L of the rib (green triangle and arrow) and continue via an easy slope and narrow channel straight to the summit (2912m/1hr 30mins from the fork/plaque at 2600m).

Descent: Go down the W ridge for about 50m and then descend a very wide gully on your L (Canalone Bissolati) that leads straight down to the Campo Pericoli slopes and traverse L here to Sella di Monte Aquila (2335m) and back to Albergo di Campo Imperatore (2130m/2hrs 15 mins).

11: Corno Grande W Summit (East Face), Canalone Centrale

Location:	Gran Sasso d'Italia
Grade:	PD+
Approach ascent:	530m
Climbing:	250m
Character:	Snow to 45° and some mixed ground.

Less popular than the Direttissima only because it involves a longer approach. A great feeling of isolation and the Bafile bivvy hut nearby serves as a perfect base before an early morning ascent.

Approach and Description: First read Note in Winter Climb 10. Reach the slopes below the East face of Corno Grande's W summit (see Scramble 2: Tour of Corno Grande) and climb to the bottom of the evident gully on the far R side of the East face. Climb the gully, keeping R where it narrows, then L where the gully is blocked. Towards the top when you reach a chimney go L up a ramp and then to the summit (2hrs from the bottom of the gully).

Descent: See Winter Climb 10.

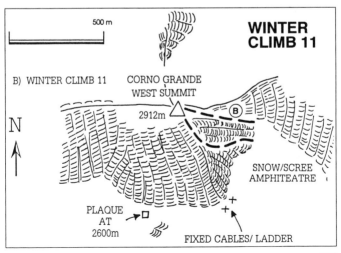

WINTER CLIMB 11

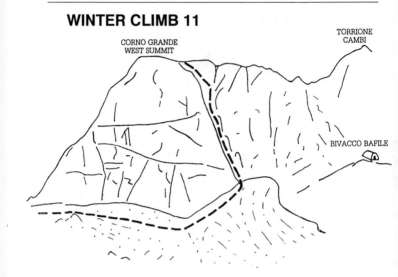

12: Corno Piccolo (North Face), Canale Sivitilli

Location:	Gran Sasso d'Italia
Grade:	PD
Approach ascent:	190m
Climbing:	450m
Character:	Snow to 50°.

Approach and Description: From La Madonnina chair-lift station (2015m) walk up the wide path past the Madonna shrine to 2060m and go R here traversing the slopes below the North face of Corno Piccolo for approx. 1km. The Canale Sivitilli gully is the one between the North face of Corno Piccolo and the rounded North face of Prima Spalla (see sketch). Climb the gully intuitively, going R at the top to reach the W ridge of Corno Piccolo (2580m) and follow this L all the way up to the summit (2hrs 45mins from La Madonnina). **Descent:** Either the route of ascent or the Via Normale down the South face (see Scramble 3: Via Danesi / Via Normale).

WINTER CLIMB 12

Il Paretone (winter)

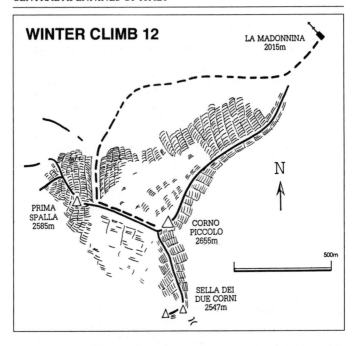

SPORT CLIMBS

Ferentillo and Grotti are two of Italy's finest sport climbing areas and it only takes an hour to drive from one to the other. Ferentillo, situated at the southern entrance of the beautiful Valnerina valley, has over 200 routes of solid limestone from (French) grade 3 to 8c. This charming corner of Umbria boasts rugged, bottle-green valleys and medieval hill villages, yet does not see all the tourists that flock to nearby Assisi, Spoleto and Perugia. An indoor climbing wall near the village is now being built and there are flood-lights at the Arrone sector, so it is possible to climb after dark in the summer. Grotti only has 50 choice routes and most of these are hard, but if you are able to climb grade 7, then pay this area a visit - you will not regret it!

Sport climber on La matematica é un opinione (6b) at Le Mummie sector, Ferentillo (see route 56).

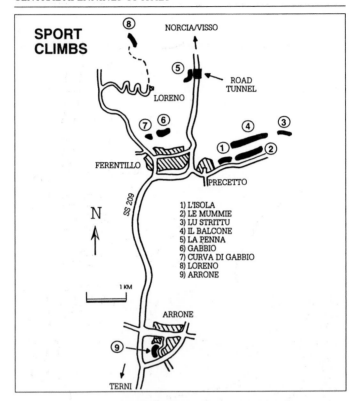

FERENTILLO

Location: 18km from Terni along the SS 209 road
               (see Map above).

SECTORS

1. L'ISOLA
How to get there: Reach Precetto village and continue towards
Monterivoso. The wall is 150m after Precetto on the L.

1.   Cindy: 5+ (20m)
2.   L'urlo di trapanetor: 6b+ (27m)

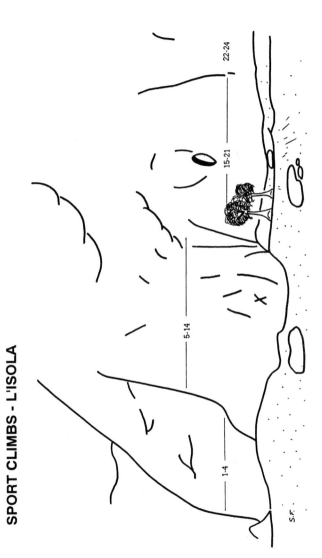

3. Ale' compagno Lobanoski: 7b (18m)
4. Classica e' bello: 6b+ (27m)
5. Antar: 6a+ (25m)
6. Itaca: 5+ (25m)
7. Il Celtico: 5+ (25m)
8. Il canto della terra: 5+ (26m), 2nd pitch: 6a+ (16m)
9. Le mele della bionda: 5/5+ (26m), 2nd pitch: 4+ (18m)
10. Viva Remo: 6a (28m), 2nd pitch: 5/5+ (29m)
11. Scusa Remo: 6a (27m)
12. Silvia ti amo: 5+/6a (27m)
13. Forza Remo: 6a (28m)
14. E' fatta: 6c (28m)
15. Blow up: 4+/5 (18m)
16. Gli insetti preferiscono le ortiche: 4+ (19m)
17. Eccola di nuovo 5+/6a (18m), 2nd pitch: 5/5+ (26m)
18. Come? 5+/6a (22m), 2nd pitch: 5 (18m)
19. Meglio tardi che mais: 6a (12m)
20. Il compleanno di Janna: 5+ (40m)
21. Geremia il cane spia: 5+/6a (18m)
22. Tienti forte scatafascio: 5+/6a (16m)
23. La pagella di Lory: 6b (16m)
24. La spada nella roccia: 6a+ (16m)

2. LE MUMMIE

How to get there: 100m beyond L'Isola sector on the L. A path leads past an old house and up to the walls.

25. La Nord dell'Aigor: 5+ (10m)
26. Remedios: 5+ (10m)
27. Aglio: 3+ (10m)
28. Olio: 3 (9m)
29. Bukarin: 7a (20m)
30. L'opera al nero: 6c (25m)
31. Zenone: 7a+ (24m)
32. Tul Tul: 5+ (27m)
33. Single: 6b (26m)
34. Glasnost: 7b (16m)
35. La signora e' servita: 6c (20m)

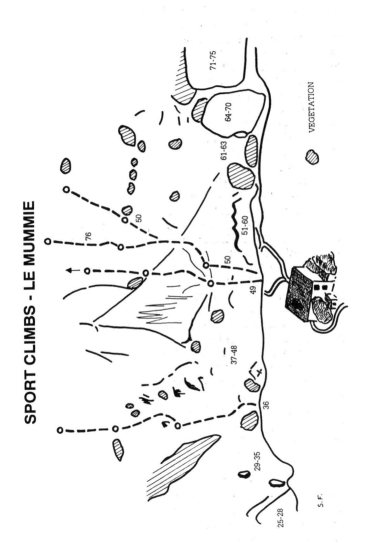

125

36. Uragano: 6a (22m), 2nd pitch: 5+ (27m),
       3rd pitch: 5/5+ (27m)
37. Il sacro Lingam: 6c (25m)
38. Zizzania: 6a+ (20m)
39. Franando: 6a (22m)
40. Federicca: 6a (20m)
41. Wang: 6a+ (20m)
42. Tovaric: 6a+ (22m)
43. Bang: 5/5+ (22m)
44. Nausica: 5/5+ (10m)
45. Circe: 5+ (10m)
46. Athena: 5+ (10m)
47. Penelope: 5/5+ (10m)
48. Pesce d'Aprile: 4+ (10m)
49. Le Ragazze: 6a (23m), 2nd pitch: 7b+ (AO) (20m),
       3rd pitch: 6b (20m), 4th pitch: 6a (23m)
50. Taxi: 6a (23m), 2nd pitch: 6a (20m), 3rd pitch: 5/5+ (15m)
51. Realizzzazzio: 8a (22m)
52. Scusate il ritardo: 7a (18m)
53. Non per soldi: 8a (18m)
54. Pace in Palestina: 7c (18m)
55. Passeggiando sul nero: 7a+ (20m)
56. La matematica è un opinione: 6b (20m)
57. Latte e B.: 6a+ (18m)
58. Burro e marmellata: 5+ (18m)
59. Pane e orzo: 5+ (18m)
60. Fiocchi d'avena: 5/5+ (18m)
61. Savinik: 7b (22m)
62. Ragazzo rosso: 7b (20m)
63. Ciato spacciato: 5+ (35m)
64. C'est ci bon: 5+/6a (20m)
65. Giulia's lovers: 6c (12m)
66. Katmandhu: 6c (13m)
67. Nada mas: 6c (13m)
68. Occhi di cane azzurro: 6c (12m)
69. Il pane e le rose: 6a+ (12m)
70. Arangetevi: 5+ (12m)
71. Cascia 90: 5+ (22m)

72.   Opera immane: 5/5+ (27m)
73.   Mal di denti: 5+/6a (24m)
74.   Pipistrelli: 6a+ (24m)
75.   Mummie sprint: 5+ (24m)
76.   Vuoto compreso: 6a (20m) starts from the first pitch lower-off point of Taxi and follows the first 5 bolts of Taxi's 2nd pitch before going direct up a chimney crack.
            2nd pitch: 6b+ (20m)

3. LU STRITTU

How to get there: From Precetto village drive E towards Monterivoso passing the L'Isola and Le Mummie sectors on your L and park where the road passes between two vertical walls (300m from Precetto). Follow the path L (sectors indicated) up through the woods turning R at a fork for Lu Strittu or continuing straight to Il Balcone (10mins walk from parking area).

77.   A' sciantosa: 5 (20m)
78.   Tammurriata: 5+ (20m)
79.   Spingola Francese: 5+/6a (20m)
80.   Variante di Settembre: 6a+ (20m)
81.   Rocky Horror: 6b (22m)

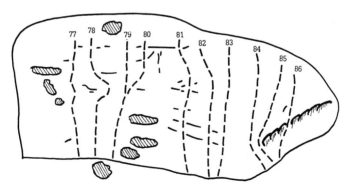

SPORT CLIMBS - LU STRITTU

82. O' Sarracino: 6a (22m)
83. Attenti al lupo: 5+/6a (22m)
84. Futura: 5+ (22m)
85. Don Raffaele: 6a (18m)
86. Chicos: 6b+ (18m)

4. IL BALCONE

How to get there: see Sector 3 - Lu Strittu

87. Piaceri particolari: 6a+ (14m)
88. Viaggio di nozze: 5+ (14m)
89. Avide lingue: 6a+ (16m)
90. Sirio: 6a (18m)
91. A mano libera: 6b+ (20m)
92. Danza con la panza: 6c+ (20m)
93. Tecnica e tigna: 6a+ (18m)
94. Sesso e tortellini: 6b (22m)
95. L'ombra del sole: 6a+ (25m)
96. Variante Orizzonti perduti: 6b+ (10m)
97. L'escalera: 6b (22m)
98. Variante virus: 6b (17m)
99. Aldebaran: 6b (18m)
100. Vega: 5+ (16m)
101. Altair: 6b (16m)
102. Hemis: 6b (25m)
103. Elena fusion: 7b+ (25m)
104. Il ritorno di Alfredo Alfredo: 7a (27m)
105. Sentieri nel ghiaccio: 6a+ (27m)
106. Certezze: 6a (22m)
107. Abbi dubbi: 6a+ (20m)
108. Zorro: 5 (18m)
109. In bocca al lupo: 7a+ (20m)
110. Super Trash: 8a (20m)
111. Super Fly: 7c (18m)
112. Savinik atto 2: 7b+ (20m)
113. Troppo allenamento: 7a+ (16m)
114. La principessa sul pisello: 7c (15m)
115. Alfredo Alfredo contro tutti: 6b+ (18m)
116. Specchio di faglia: 6a (22m)

SPORT CLIMBS - IL BALCONE

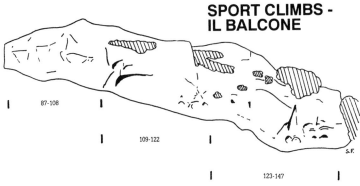

117. Le mutande di sicurezza: 6a (27m)
118. Ricomincio da zero: 5/5+ (18m)
119. A' livella: 5+ (18m)
120. Acquarium Dei: 6b+ (18m)
121. Freesby: 6a+ (18m)
122. Luna comanche: 6b+ (20m)
123. Ipotesi teologica sul mare: 6a+ (16m)
124. Sai Pen: 6a (16m)
125. Work shop: 6b (18m)
126. Il diedro dei lunghi coltelli: 6a (20m)
127. La zozza: 6c (18m)
128. Palla strizzolina: 7a (20m)
129. La rabbia esaurita: 6c (20m)
130. La rabbia esaudita: 6c+ (20m)
131. Born to climb: 8a (27m)
132. Slavo: 6b (10m)
133. Nononano: 6a+ (10m)
134. La route du Rome: 7b+ (28m)
135. Arabesque: 6b (27m)
136. Noblesse obligue: 6b+ (26m)
137. Critica all'inerzia conoscitiva: 7a+ (26m)
138. Maudit: 7b+ (26m)
139. Luna rossa: 7b+ (26m)
140. Mago 89: 7a+ (15m)
141. Aquila della notte: 7b+ (15m)

*The 'organ pipes' of
Freesby (6a+) at
Il Bacone, Ferentillo.
Route 121*

142.   Bird: 8a (14m)
143.   Il Re del mondo: 7c (18m)
144.   I vulcaniani: 7a+ (21m)
145.   Ferentillo climbing: 7a+ (20m)
146.   Ricci e i suoi capricci: 6b (18m)
147.   Navajo: 5+ (18m)

5. LA PENNA

How to get there: From Ferentillo drive N up the Valnerina (SS 209)
for approx. 2.5km where the road passes through a short, open

tunnel. Routes 148-157 are situated on the L of the tunnel and you have to climb over a low barbed wire fence (this is private property, but open to considerate climbers). Routes 158-161 start inside the tunnel on the L and the remaining routes begin from the roof of the tunnel.

148. Me piacerebbe: 7c (20m)
149. Gaudi: 7c (22m)
150. Perestrojka: 7b+ (18m)
151. Broncos: 7b+ (18m)
152. Me' morto il gatto: 7a (15m)
153. Pecos Bill: 7a+ (15m)
154. Mummia: 7a (8m)
155. Cadavere: 6b+ (10m)
156. Hobbit: 6a+ (20m)
157. Laralalla': 6c (18m)
158. Dramma: 7b (15m)
159. Ho azzardato troppo: 7b+ (15m)
160. Hata climb: 7b (20m)
161. Escluso dal giro: 7c+ (18m)
162. L'isola dei tre: 5+ (15m)
163. 20. 000 lire sulla strada: 5/5+ (15m)
164. Vota bene: 5/5+ (15m)
165. Ai confini della mozzarella: 7b+ (18m)
166. C.C.C.P.: 7b (18m)
167. Ciccio bello: 6a (15m), 2nd pitch: 8a (15m)

6. GABBIO

How to get there: Take the rough road opposite Ferentillo church to the semi-deserted village of Gabbio (1.5km). Walk through the village and turn R along a path for 200m before climbing a little wall on your L and then crossing a small olive grove. A path leads up to the cave.

168. Hei sei: 6b+ (18m)
169. Maledetti vi odio: 6c+ (18m)
170. Uomo civile: 8a+ (18m)
171. Portatore di tempesta: 7c+ (20m)
172. So sexi: 8a+ (20m)

173.   Nel buio: 8b (25m)
174.   Calvizia: 7b+ (25m)
175.   Troppa informazione: 7b (25m)
176.   Il sentiero dei giganti: 7a+ (25m)
177.   Bombardamentos: 5+/6a (18m)
178.   Alfredo Alfredo: 5/5+ (18m), 2nd pitch: 7b (20m)
179.   Polpastrillo: 5+ (18m)
180.   Tex Mex: 5/5+ (18m), 2nd pitch: 6b (7m)
181.   Zambia Italia 4-0: 6a+ (16m)
182.   Lo spigolo delle streghe: 6b (15m)
183.   Romeo 89: 7a+ (18m)
184.   Il morbo di Ciato: 7b+ (18m)
185.   Mandela superstar: 7c+ (18m)
186.   The Chinese way: 7b (18m)
187.   Prosciuttini: 6c (18m)
188.   Donne in amore: 6a+ (18m)
189.   Rock a gay'n: 7a (15m)
190.   Mumble mumble: 6a+ (18m)
191.   Hare Krisna: 6a (18m)
192.   Yuk Baluk: 6b+ (18m)
193.   Fragole e sangue: 6b (18m)

7. CURVA DI GABBIO
How to get there: Follow the path from the last bend before reaching Gabbio village.
194.   Pinco Panco: 7a+ (15m)
195.   5-10-88 Viva Chile: 6c (18m)
196.   Viaggio automatico: 7b+ (18m)
197.   Viaggio segreto: 8b+ (12m)
198.   Abbasso le Olimpiadi: 7b (18m)
199.   Ruby: 7c+ (18m)

8. LORENO
How to get there: From Ferentillo take the road signposted Ancaiano for a few kilometres as far as a junction signposted "Nicciano/Loreno" and drive through both of these villages. A rough track

SPORT CLIMBS
LORENO

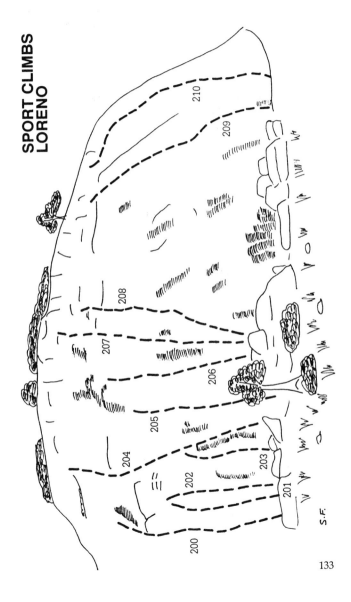

(1.5km) leads to a derelict building. The crag is 10mins walk through woods (L) above a pine forest enclosure from there.

200.	Difficilina: 6b+ (15m)
201.	La Pantera: 7a (12m)
202.	Apoye: 7b (12m)
203.	Ombre nella pioggia: 7b (20m)
204.	Lianxi Tek: 7a+ (8m Variant start to "Ombre")
205.	Top secret: 7b (12m)
206.	Liberati's tragedy: 7a+ (12m)
207.	Fut: 7c (18m)
208.	Pa Xi Loung: 8a (15m)
209.	Keng: 8c (probably) (18m)
210.	Lianxi Mah: 7a+ (18m)

9. ARRONE

How to get there: Take the road S from Ferentillo to Arrone (5km) and go through Arrone, turning R to pass the "municipio" (modern, yellow building) and arrive at the crag.

211.	Lo sfrondatore: 5 (15m)
212.	Bianca: 4+ (16m)
213.	Sotto il segno dei peschi: 6b (14m)
214.	Cachi express: 5 (11m)
215.	Rinvia sul fico: 5 (11m)
216.	La Sfinge: 6a (25m)
217.	The Who: 5 (12m)
218.	Oro, incenso e mirro: 5 (12m), 2nd pitch: 6b (17m)
219.	Tornado: 5+/6a (12m), 2nd pitch: 6c (12m)
220.	Tiramisu': 6a+ (22m)
221.	Orrizonte: 6b (20m)
222.	Expedition: 6b+ (22m)
223.	Tequila sunrise: 6c+ (20m)
224.	La rabbia degli angeli: 7b+ (22m)
225.	Pinball wizard: 7a+ (22m)
226.	Il sole buio: 7b (20m)
227.	Peter Pan: 5+/6a (20m)
228.	Red Skorpion: 5+ (18m)
229.	Wong Long: 6a+ (18m)
230.	Arrone climbing: 6a (18m)

GROTTI

Location: 10km SE of Rieti along the SS 578 road.
Iniziazione is the first crag you reach after ascending the
steep path from the parking area by a sports shop (10mins)
and all the other sectors are situated to the R of this (see Map
28).

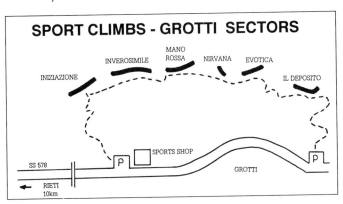

SECTORS

1. INIZIAZIONE

1.   Snoby: 5 (8m)
2.   Il nervoso: 5 (8m)
3.   Gladio: 6a (10m)
4.   Gladiatori: 6b (10m)
5.   ?: 6b+ (10m)
6.   Reve d'un amour: 7c (18m)
7.   Iniziazione: 7b (18m)
8.   Balla coi buchi: 7c (18m)
9.   Buco ben fatto: 7b+ (16m)
10.   Boys scraus: 7c (18m)
11.   S.P.Q.R.: 7a+ (16m)
12.   El Grinta: 6c (14m)

SPORT CLIMBS - INIZIAZIONE

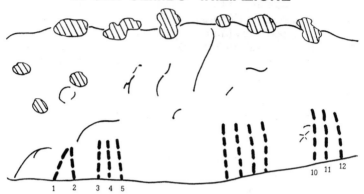

2. INVEROSIMILE

13.	Nome segreto: 7a+ (20m)
14.	Grigio pirla: 7a+ (20m)
15.	Blob: 7a+ (20m)
16.	Ouzo power: 7b+ (23m)
17.	Bee beep: 7c (25m)
18.	Lupo de lupis: 8a (28m)
19.	Terima Kasih: 7a (18m), 2nd pitch: 7b+ (10m)

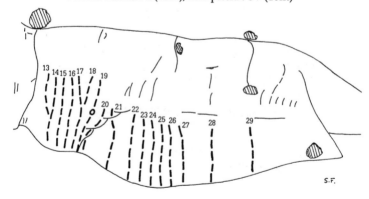

SPORT CLIMBS - INVEROSIMILE

20.   Eu: 7c+ (18m)
21.   Ridi mo': 8b (18m)
22.   Kingston: 7c+ (20m)
23.   Seiccippiu': 7b+ (20m)
24.   Pancio cherubino: 7c (20m)
25.   Pink rabbit: 8a (22m)
26.   Fatos: 7c+ (23m)
27.   Assalto frontale: 8a+ (23m)
28.   Umore e depressione: 7c+ (20m)
29.   Frustami: 7b (16m)

3. MANO ROSSA

30.   La mano rossa: 8a (25m)
31.   Senza tregua: 7c (22m)
32.   Il gran troncadero: 7c (22m)
33.   Requiem: 7b+ (22m)

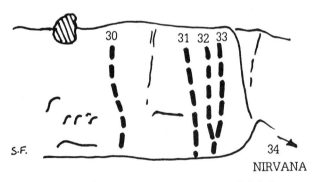

SPORT CLIMBS - MANO ROSSA

4. NIRVANA

34.   Nirvana: 8b (12m)

5. EROTICA

35. ?: 6c (10m)
36. Viva Gimbo: 7a (18m)
37. Never mind: 6c+ (18m)
38. Acid jazz: 7b (18m)
39. Il corpo di Cristo: 7b (18m)
40. Rigurgito: 7c+ (15m)
41. Erotica: 8a+ (10m)

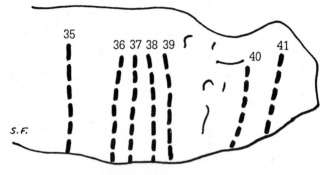

SPORT CLIMBS - EROTICA

6. IL DEPOSITO

42. Dinamite bla: 6c+ (15m)
43. Nonna Papera: 7a+ (15m)
44. LA 313: 7b (15m)
45. Gambadilegno: 7a+ (15m)
46. AK 47: 7b (15m)
47. Filo sganga: 7c+ (15m)
48. Qui quo qua: 8b (15m)
49. La riscossa dei Bassotti: 8a (12m)
50. L'Ispettore Manetta: 7c (10m)

SPORT CLIMBS - IL DEPOSITO

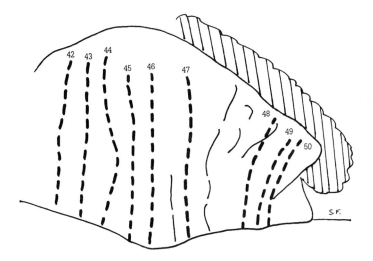

CICERONE GUIDES to WALKING IN SWITZERLAND & ITALY
and adjacent Alpine areas

ALPINE PASS ROUTE, SWITZERLAND *Kev Reynolds* Over 15 passes along the northern edge of the Alps, past the Eiger, Jungfrau and many other renowned peaks. *ISBN 1 85284 069 2   176pp   £6.99*

THE BERNESE ALPS, SWITZERLAND *Kev Reynolds* Includes walks around Grindelwald, Lauterbrunnen and Kandersteg dominated by the great peaks of the Oberland. *ISBN 1 85284 074 9   248pp PVC cover Temp out of print. Update in preparation 1997.*

CENTRAL SWITZERLAND - A Walking Guide *Kev Reynolds* A delightful area stretching from Luzern to the St Gotthard, includes Engelberg and Klausen Pass. *ISBN 1 85284 131 1   216pp PVC cover   £10.99*

CHAMONIX to ZERMATT The Walker's Haute Route *Kev Reynolds* The classic walk in the shadow of great peaks from Mont Blanc to the Matterhorn. *ISBN 1 85284 215 6   176pp   £7.99*

WALKS IN THE ENGADINE, SWITZERLAND *Kev Reynolds* The superb country of the Bregaglia, Bernina Alps, and the National Park. *ISBN 1 85284 003 X   192pp   PVC cover   £8.99*

THE JURA: WALKING THE HIGH ROUTE *Kev Reynolds* **WINTER SKI TRAVERSES** *R.Brian Evans* The High Route is a long distance path along the highest crest of the Swiss Jura. In winter the area is a paradise for walkers on cross-country skis. *ISBN 1 85284 010 2   192pp   £6.99*

WALKING IN TICINO, SWITZERLAND *Kev Reynolds.* Walks in the lovely Italian part of Switzerland, surprisingly little known to British walkers. *ISBN 1 85284 098 6   184pp PVC cover £9.99*

THE VALAIS, SWITZERLAND. A Walking Guide *Kev Reynolds* The splendid scenery of the Pennine Alps, with such peaks as the Matterhorn, Dent Blanche, and Mont Rosa, providing a perfect background. *ISBN 1 85284 151 6   224pp   PVC cover   £11.99*

THE GRAND TOUR OF MONTE ROSA *C.J.Wright*

Vol 1 - Martigny to Valle della Sesia (via the Italian valleys) *ISBN 1 85284 177 X   216pp   £14.99*
Vol 2 - Valle della Sesia to Martigny (via the Swiss valleys) *ISBN 1 85284 178 8 182pp £14.99* The ultimate alpine LD walk which encircles most of the Pennine Alps.

ALTA VIA - HIGH LEVEL WALKS IN THE DOLOMITES *Martin Collins* Two of the most popular mountain paths in Europe - Alta Via 1 and 2. *ISBN 0 902363 75 1   160pp   PVC cover   £8.99*

THE CENTRAL APENNINES OF ITALY Walks, Scrambles and Climbs *Stephen Fox* The mountainous spine of Italy, with secluded walks, rock climbs and scrambles on the Gran Sasso d'Italia, and some of Italy's finest sport climbing crags. *ISBN 1 85284 219 9*

ITALIAN ROCK. Selected Climbs in Northern Italy *Al Churcher.* Val d'Orco and Mello, Lecco and Finale etc. *ISBN 0 902363 93 X   200pp   PVC cover   £8.99*

VIA FERRATA SCRAMBLES IN THE DOLOMITES *Höfler/Werner Translated by Cecil Davies.* The most exciting walks in the world. Wires, stemples and ladders enable the 'walker' to enter the climber's vertical environment. *ISBN 1 85284 089 7 248pp PVC cover £10.99*

WALKING IN THE CENTRAL ITALIAN ALPS *Gillian Price* Vinschgau, Ortler and Adamello regions. Little known to British walkers, certain to become popular *ISBN 1 85284 183 4 230pp PVC cover £10.99*

WALKING IN THE DOLOMITES *Gillian Price* A comprehensive selection of walks amongst spectacular rock scenery. By far the best English guide to the area. *ISBN 1 85284 079 X PVC cover £10.99*

WALKS IN THE JULIAN ALPS *Simon Brown* Slovenia contains some of Europe's most attractive mountain limestone scenery. 30 walks as an introduction to the area, from valley strolls to high mountain scrambles. *ISBN 1 85284 125 7   184pp   £8.99*

THERE ARE CICERONE GUIDES TO MANY OTHER COUNTRIES

THE BRITTANY COASTAL PATH *Alan Castle* The GR34, 360 miles takes a month to walk. Easy access from UK means it can be split into several holidays. *ISBN 1 85284 185 0 296pp £10.99*

CHAMONIX- MONT BLANC - A Walking Guide *Martin Collins* In the dominating presence of Europe's highest mountain, the scenery is exceptional. *ISBN 1 85284 009 9 192pp PVC cover £8.99*

THE CORSICAN HIGH LEVEL ROUTE - Walking the GR20 *Alan Castle* The most challenging of the French LD paths - across the rocky spine of Corsica. *ISBN 1 85284 100 1 104pp £5.99*

FRENCH ROCK *Bill Birkett* THE guide to many exciting French crags! Masses of photo topos, with selected hit-routes in detail. *ISBN 1 85284 113 3. 332pp A5 size. £14.99*

THE PYRENEAN TRAIL: GR10 *Alan Castle* From the Atlantic to the Mediterranean at a lower level than the Pyrenean High Route. 50 days but splits into holiday sections. *ISBN 1 85284 038 2 Update 1997.*

THE ROBERT LOUIS STEVENSON TRAIL *Alan Castle* 140 mile trail in the footsteps of Stevenson's "Travels with a Donkey" through the Cevennes. *ISBN 1 85284 060 9 160pp £7.99*

Selected ROCK CLIMBS IN BELGIUM & LUXEMBOURG *Chris Craggs* Perfect rock, good protection and not too hot to climb in summer. *ISBN 1 85284 155 9 188p A5 £12.99*

ROCK CLIMBS IN THE VERDON. An Introduction *Rick Newcombe* An English-style guide, which makes for easier identification of the routes and descents. *ISBN 1 85284 015 3 72pp £5.50*

TOUR OF MONT BLANC *Andrew Harper* One of the world's best walks - the circumnavigation of the Mont Blanc massif. *ISBN 1 85284 011 0 144pp PVC cover Update in preparation*

TOUR OF THE OISANS: GR54 *Andrew Harper* This popular walk around the massif is similar in quality to the celebrated Tour of Mont Blanc. *ISBN 1 85284 157 5 120pp PVC cover £9.99*

THE TOUR OF THE QUEYRAS *Alan Castle* A 13 day walk on the GR58 and GR541 which traverses wild but beautiful country, the sunniest part of the French Alps. Eminently suitable for a first Alpine visit. *ISBN 1 85284 048 X 160pp £6.99*

TOUR OF THE VANOISE *Kev Reynolds* A circuit of one of the finest mountain areas of France. The second most popular mountain tour after the Tour of Mont Blanc. *ISBN 1 85284 224 5 120pp £7.99*

WALKING IN THE ARDENNES *Alan Castle* The Belgian provinces of Namur, Luxembourg and Liege are a mecca for outdoor enthusiasts. Gorges and deep cut wooded valleys, caves, castles and hundreds of walking trails. *ISBN 1 85284 213 X 312pp £12.99*

WALKING THE FRENCH ALPS: GR5 *Martin Collins* The popular From Lake Geneva to Nice. Split into stages, each of which could form the basis of a good holiday. *ISBN 1 85284 051 X 160pp £8.99*

WALKING THE FRENCH GORGES *Alan Castle* 320 miles through Provence and Ardèche, includes the famous gorges of the Verdon. *ISBN 1 85284 114 1 224pp £7.99*

WALKING IN THE HAUTE SAVOIE *Janette Norton* 61 walks in the lovely pre-Alps of Chablais, to majestic peaks in the Faucigny, Haut Giffre and Lake Annecy regions. *ISBN 1 85284 196 6 312pp £12.99*

WALKING IN THE TARENTAISE & BEAUFORTAIN ALPS *J.W. Akitt* The delectable mountain area south of Mont Blanc includes the Vanoise National Park. 53 day walks, 5 tours between 2 and 8 days duration, plus 40 short outings. *ISBN 1 85284 181 8 216pp £9.99*

WALKS IN VOLCANO COUNTRY *Alan Castle* Two LD walks in Central France- the High Auvergne and Tour of the Velay - in a unique landscape of extinct volcanoes. *ISBN 1 85284 092 7 208pp £8.50*

THERE ARE CICERONE GUIDES TO MANY OTHER COUNTRIES
- send large s.a.e. for catalogue - 2 Police Square, Milnthorpe, Cumbria, LA7 7QE

WALKING IN THE ALGARVE *June Parker* The author of *Walking in Mallorca* turns her expert attention to the Algarve. *ISBN 1 85284 173 7 168pp £7.99*

ANDALUSIAN ROCK CLIMBS *Chris Craggs* El Chorro and El Torcal are world famous. Includes Tenerife. *ISBN 1 85284 109 5 168pp £6.99*

BIRDWATCHING IN MALLORCA *Ken Stoba* Did you know Mallorca was a birdwatching paradise? A complete guide to what to see and where to see it. *ISBN 1 85284 053 6 108pp £5.50*

COSTA BLANCA CLIMBS *Chris Craggs* Fantastic routes on sun-drenched rock. Now one of Europe's most popular climbing areas. *New much enlarged edition in preparation*

MOUNTAIN WALKS ON THE COSTA BLANCA *Bob Stansfield* An easily accessible winter walking paradise to rival Mallorca. *ISBN1 85284 165 6 232pp £9.99*

ROCK CLIMBS IN MAJORCA, IBIZA & TENERIFE *Chris Craggs* Holiday island cragging at its best. *ISBN 1 85284 189 3 240pp £10.99*

WALKING IN MALLORCA *June Parker* Away from the tourist fleshpots, Mallorca possesses striking limestone peaks and magnificent walks. Ideal for a winter sunshine break. *ISBN 1 85284 078 1 264pp PVC cover £11.99*

THE MOUNTAINS OF CENTRAL SPAIN *Jaqueline Oglesby* Walks and scrambles in the Sierras de Gredos and Guadarrama which rise to 2600m and are snow capped for five months of the year. *ISBN 1 85284 203 2 312p £14.99*

THROUGH THE SPANISH PYRENEES: GR11 *Paul Lucia* A new long distance trail which mirrors the French GR10 but traverses much lonelier, wilder country *ISBN 1 85284 222 9 232pp £9.99*

WALKING IN THE SIERRA NEVADA *Andy Walmsley* Spain's highest mountain range is a wonderland for the traveller,wilderness backpacker or mountain biker. *ISBN 1 85284 194 X 160pp £8.99*

WALKS & CLIMBS IN THE PICOS DE EUROPA *Robin Walker* A definitive guide to these unique mountains. Walks and rock climbs of all grades. *ISBN 1 85284 033 1 232pp PVC cover £10.99*

THE WAY OF ST JAMES: SPAIN *Alison Raju* The popular Pilgrim Road from the Pyrenees to Santiago de Compostela. Includes other Spanish Pilgrim routes. *ISBN 1 85284 142 7 152pp £7.99*

ROCK CLIMBS IN THE PYRENEES *Derek Walker* Impressive climbs on Pic du Midi d'Ossau and the Vignemale in France;the Ordesa Canyon and Riglos in Spain.*ISBN 1 85284 039 0 168pp PVC cover £9.99*

WALKS & CLIMBS IN THE PYRENEES *Kev Reynolds* Includes the Pyrenean High Level Route. Invaluable for any backpacker or mountaineer who plans to visit this still unspoilt mountain range. (3rd Edition) *ISBN 1 85284 133 8 328pp PVC cover £14.99*

THE ATLAS MOUNTAINS *Karl Smith* Trekking in the mountains of north Africa. Practical and comprehensive. *ISBN 1 85284 032 3 136pp PVC cover £9.99*

CRETE OFF THE BEATEN TRACK *Bruce and Naomi Caughey* Short walks, mountain hikes, gorges, coves and beaches. Ruins of ancient civilizations abound. *ISBN 1 85284 019 6 152pp £7.99*

WALKING IN CYPRUS *Donald Brown* Without a guide, getting lost in Cyprus is easy. Donald Brown shares undiscovered Cyprus with walkers *ISBN 1 85284 195 8 144pp £8.99*

THE MOUNTAINS OF GREECE. A Walker's Guide *Tim Salmon* Hikes of all grades from a month-long traverse of the Pindos to day hikes on the outskirts of Athens. *ISBN 1 85284 108 7 PVC cover £9.99*

THE MOUNTAINS OF TURKEY *Karl Smith* Over 100 treks and scrambles with detailed route descriptions of all the popular peaks. Includes Ararat. *ISBN 1 85284 161 3 184pp PVC cover £14.99*

TREKS AND CLIMBS in WADI RUM, JORDAN *Tony Howard* An amazing treasure house of climbing and trekking. *ISBN 1 85284 135 4 204pp A5 Card cover £12.99*

THE ALA DAG, Climbs and Treks in Turkey's Crimson Mountains *O.B.Tüzel* The best mountaineering area in Turkey. Destined to be one of the in-places. *ISBN 1 85284 112 5 296pp PVC cover £14.99*

PRINTED BY CARNMOR PRINT & DESIGN
95/97 LONDON ROAD, PRESTON, LANCASHIRE